A DEFENSE of HUME on MIRACLES

—————————————•¶MP•—————————————

PRINCETON MONOGRAPHS
IN PHILOSOPHY

Harry Frankfurt, Editor

——————————·ꟼMP·——————————

The Princeton Monographs in Philosophy series
offers short historical and systematic studies
on a wide variety of philosophical topics.

Justice Is Conflict by STUART HAMPSHIRE

Liberty Worth the Name by GIDEON YAFFE

Self-Deception Unmasked by ALFRED R. MELE

Public Goods, Private Goods by RAYMOND GEUSS

Welfare and Rational Care by STEPHEN DARWALL

A Defense of Hume on Miracles by ROBERT FOGELIN

A DEFENSE of HUME
on MIRACLES

Robert J. Fogelin

PRINCETON UNIVERSITY PRESS

PRINCETON AND OXFORD

Copyright © 2003 by Princeton University Press
Published by Princeton University Press, 41 William Street,
Princeton, New Jersey 08540

In the United Kingdom: Princeton University Press, 3 Market Place,
Woodstock, Oxfordshire OX20 1SY

Library of Congress Cataloging-in-Publication Data

Fogelin, Robert J.
A defense of Hume on miracles / Robert J. Fogelin.
p. cm. — (Princeton monographs in philosophy)
Includes bibliographical references and index.
ISBN 0-691-11430-7 (alk. paper)
1. Hume, David, 1711–1776. 2. Miracles. I. Title. II. Series.
B1499.M5 F64 2003
212—dc21   2002042466

British Library Cataloging-in-Publication Data is available

This book has been composed in Janson Text with Centaur Display
Printed on acid-free paper ∞
www.pupress.princeton.edu
Printed in the United States of America
1 3 5 7 9 10 8 6 4 2

For my son, Eric

Crowds flocking to the grave of a Jansenist priest credited with

miraculous healing powers actually ate dirt from the grave, and

threatened to get out of hand. When the cemetery was barred

off by the authorities, a sign appeared inscribed:

De par le roi défense à Dieu

De faire miracle en ce lieu.

(By order of the king, God is forbidden

to perform miracles in this place.)

—*Encyclopedia of Philosophy,* "Enlightenment"

Contents

Preface

A NUMBER OF PEOPLE HAVE provided both encouragement and help in the creation of this work. Walter Sinnott-Armstrong read an early version and made a number of suggestions that clarified the project. The two (no longer anonymous) readers, Don Garrett and David Owen, are both distinguished Hume scholars. Together they saved me from a number of embarrassing gaffes and also pointed out important ways in which my reading of Hume and my defense of his views could be made stronger. Harry Frankfurt provided assistance of a different kind: Hesitant as he was about accepting my reading of Hume, and hardly enthusiastic about Hume's argument itself, his questions forced me to address those who are not already converts to Hume's position. James Fieser, a prodigious scholar, tracked down the exact sources of some obscure eighteenth-century arguments attacking Hume that I cite. The epigraph is a gift from Roy Sorensen.

I would also like to thank Ian Malcolm and Harry Frankfurt for seeing this project through the Princeton University Press. Florence Fogelin, Jane Taylor, and the Princeton University Press's Lauren Lepow performed wonders in civilizing the manuscript. I wish to thank the Oxford University Press for allowing me to reprint in its entirety section 10 of Hume's *Enquiry concerning Human Understanding*.

This project was supported by the research funds associated with my holding the Sherman Fairchild Professorship in the Humanities at Dartmouth College.

Abbreviations

THROUGHOUT THE BOOK references to Hume's *Enquiry concerning Human Understanding* are to the 1999 Oxford edition, edited by Tom L. Beauchamp. Citations to this text have the following form: (*EHU*, section.paragraph). For example, (*EHU*, 10.4) refers to section 10, paragraph 4 of the *Enquiry*. References to *Hume's Treatise of Human Nature* are to the 2000 Oxford edition, edited by David Fate Norton and Mary J. Norton. Citations to this text have the following form: (*THN*, book.part.section.paragraph). For example, (*THN*, 1.4.5.35) refers to book 1, part 4, section 5, paragraph 35 of the *Treatise*. This method of abbreviation reflects that used by the editors of these volumes.

A DEFENSE of HUME on MIRACLES

—————————•¶MP•—————————

Introduction

On my return from Italy, I had the mortification to find all
England in a ferment, on account of Dr. Middleton's Free
Enquiry, while my performance was entirely overlooked
and neglected.

—David Hume, *My Own Life*

THE FULL TITLE OF Thomas Middleton's *Free Inquiry* is *A Free
Inquiry into Miraculous Powers, Which are supposed to have subsisted
in the Christian Church, From the Earliest Ages through several
successive Centuries*. It is an anti-Papist tract intended to show
that Christian miracles did not continue into post-Apostolic
times and that, for this reason, none of the later miracles
claimed in support of the Roman Catholic Church should be
acknowledged. When it appeared in 1749, Middleton's work
caused a sensation, whereas David Hume's recently published
Enquiry concerning Human Understanding (1748), including its
own examination of miracles, was, as he ruefully reports, entirely overlooked and neglected. With time, the roles have re-
versed. Middleton's work (somewhat sadly) has fallen into ob-

scurity, while Hume's discussion of miracles continues to attract serious attention.

Hume's essay "Of Miracles" appears as section 10 of his *Enquiry concerning Human Understanding*. Hume had originally planned to include a discussion on this topic in his *Treatise of Human Nature* but, for reasons of prudence, decided not to do so.[1] It appears in the *Enquiry* as one of two sections on religious matters. The second, which follows it, is titled "Of a particular Providence and of a future State." Neither essay is friendly to the cause of religion. Both seem intended to be provocative. If so, at least the essay on miracles has succeeded admirably. For more than two centuries it has been an object of vigorous defense and equally vigorous (often abusive) attack.

Hume, whose confessed ruling passion was a love of literary fame, would surely be pleased by this continuing attention, but I think he would also be perplexed by the wide range of competing interpretations of his position concerning miracles. Without making claims for originality on any particular point, I will attempt to provide a coherent reading—something like a narrative—of the way the text unfolds. This is the first and primary task of this work.

My exposition of Hume's position concerning miracles turns crucially on rejecting what I take to be two common misreadings of the text—misreadings that, in various ways, feed on each other. The first misreading is that, in part 1 of his essay on miracles, Hume maintains that no testimony could ever be sufficient to establish the occurrence of a miracle. Hume does not say this in part 1. Indeed, Hume *nowhere* asserts this, though in part 2 he does say, "Upon the whole . . . it appears, that no testimony for any kind of miracle *has* ever amounted to a probability, much less to a proof" (*EHU*, 10.35, emphasis added). The second common misreading of the text is that in part 1 Hume presents what he takes to be an a priori argument sufficient by itself to establish his fundamental theses concerning the status of testimony in behalf of miracles. This, I will argue, is false.

Nor is part 2 simply an add-on containing supplementary a posteriori considerations that also bear on the topic of miracles. Part 2 is essential for the completion of the argument begun in part 1. The second task of this work is to make good these interpretive claims.

The third task is to respond specifically to attacks that Hume's treatment of miracles has encountered in recent literature. This work was provoked in part by these misguided, often ill-tempered, bashings. Its overarching goal is not, however, to engage in counterpolemics, but rather to show that Hume's treatment of miracles, when properly understood, exhibits a level of richness, subtlety, coherence, and force not generally appreciated.

I

The Structure of Hume's Argument

Standards for evaluating testimony. Hume opens his examination of miracles with a general discussion of beliefs founded on testimony.[2] He then moves quickly to apply these reflections to the special case of miracles. Perhaps Hume moves too quickly, for many commentators pay insufficient attention to these opening general reflections. Here we will proceed more slowly.

Hume begins his argument by reminding his readers of the complexity and fallibility of causal reasoning.

> Though experience be our only guide in reasoning concerning matters of fact; it must be acknowledged, that this guide is not altogether infallible, but in some cases is apt to lead us into errors. . . . All effects follow not with like certainty from their supposed causes. Some events are found, in all countries and all ages, to have been constantly conjoined together: Others are found to have been more variable, and sometimes to disappoint our expectations; so that, in our reasonings concerning matter of fact, there are all imaginable degrees of assurance, from the highest certainty to the lowest species of moral evidence. (*EHU*, 10.3)

Because of this variability, Hume tells us, "A wise man, therefore, proportions his belief to the evidence" (*EHU*, 10.4). Then, summarizing an earlier discussion of the *probability of causes* in section 6, Hume tells us, in broad strokes, how this proportioning is to be done.

> In such conclusions as are founded on an infallible experience, he expects the event with the last degree of assurance, and regards his past experience as a full *proof* of the future existence of that event. In other cases, he proceeds with more caution: He weighs the opposite experiments: He considers which side is supported by the greater number of experiments: To that side he inclines, with doubt and hesitation; and when at last he fixes his judgment, the evidence exceeds not what we properly call *probability*. All probability, then, supposes an opposition of experiments and observations; where the one side is found to overbalance the other, and to produce a degree of evidence, proportioned to the superiority. . . . In all cases, we must balance the opposite experiments, where they are opposite, and deduct the smaller number from the greater, in order to know the exact force of the superior evidence. (*EHU*, 10.4)

These remarks provide the general framework for Hume's treatment of testimony in general and, more specifically, his treatment of testimony in behalf of miracles.

Turning to testimony, Hume begins by acknowledging its importance as a source of well-founded belief:

> We may observe, that there is no species of reasoning more common, more useful, and even necessary to human life, than that which is derived from the testimony of men, and the reports of eye-witnesses and spectators. (*EHU*, 10.5)

He then goes on to claim that the evaluation of testimony, though perhaps not strictly speaking the same as the evaluation of a causal claim, is at least very much like it.

> This species of reasoning, perhaps, one may deny to be founded on the relation of cause and effect. I shall not dispute about a word. It will be sufficient to observe, that our assurance in any

argument of this kind is derived from no other principle than our observation of the veracity of human testimony, and of the usual conformity of facts to the reports of witnesses. (*EHU*, 10.5)

That is, in deciding whether a body of testimony is reliable, we should ask whether it is of a kind that usually yields conformity between facts and what are reported as facts.[3]

Hume goes on to specify two ways (or two directions) in which the evaluation of testimony can proceed. On the first approach, we focus on the quality of the reports themselves and on the qualifications of those who have offered them:

We entertain a suspicion concerning any matter of fact, when the witnesses contradict each other; when they are but few, or of a doubtful character; when they have an interest in what they affirm; when they deliver their testimony with hesitation, or on the contrary, with too violent asseverations. There are many other particulars of the same kind, which may diminish or destroy the force of any argument, derived from human testimony. (*EHU*, 10.7)

Here we examine the testimony for the standard marks of unreliability that Hume lists. When such marks of unreliability are present, we rightly become suspicious concerning the quality of the testimony. We will call this the *direct* test for evaluating testimony.

Hume suggests a second method for evaluating testimony, this time concentrating on the nature of the *event* attested to.

Suppose, for instance, that the fact, which the testimony endeavours to establish, partakes of the extraordinary and the marvellous; in that case, the evidence, resulting from the testimony, admits of a diminution, greater or less, in proportion as the fact is more or less unusual. The reason, why we place any credit in witnesses and historians, is not derived from any *connexion*, which we perceive *a priori*, between testimony and reality, but because we are accustomed to find a conformity between them. But when the fact attested is such a one as has seldom fallen under our observation, here is a contest of two opposite experiences; of which the one destroys the other, as far as its force goes, and the superior can only operate on the mind by the force, which remains. The very same principle of experience, which gives us a certain degree of assurance in the testimony of witnesses, gives us also, in this case, another degree of assurance against the fact, which they endeavour to establish; from which contradiction there necessarily arises a counterpoise, and mutual destruction of belief and authority.

I should not believe such a story were it told me by CATO; was a proverbial saying in ROME, even during the lifetime of that philosophical patriot. The incredibility of a fact, it was allowed, might invalidate so great an authority. (*EHU*, 10.8–9)

Here we proceed in the opposite way from that used in the direct test. We start by considering the probability that a reported event could have occurred without taking into account the testimony given in its behalf. If an event is extraordinary or marvelous, then, to repeat Hume's exact words, "the evidence, resulting from the testimony, admits of a diminution, greater or less, in proportion as the fact is more or less unusual." Here the improbability of the event's occurring gives us some (though perhaps not decisive) grounds for challenging the force of the testimony. We will call this the *reverse* method of evaluating testimony.

It is clear that Hume does not invoke either of these methods in support of a general skepticism concerning testimony; indeed, in this discussion his radical skeptical arguments are kept securely on the shelf. Adopting what he takes to be common standards, Hume raises no objections to testimony in behalf of events of an *ordinary* kind, offered by *competent* witnesses having no motives to *deceive*. Here Hume's discussion of testimony closely parallels one found in John Locke's *Essay concerning Human Understanding*. There Locke remarks that "in things that happen indifferently, as that a bird should fly this or that way; that it should thunder on a man's right or left hand, &c.

when any particular matter of fact is vouched by the concurrent testimony of unsuspected witnesses, there our assent is . . . unavoidable" (Locke 1979, bk. 4, chap. 16, sec. 8). Locke then adds this cautionary note:

> The difficulty is, when testimonies contradict common experience, and the reports of history and witnesses clash with the ordinary course of nature, or with one another; there it is, where diligence, attention, and exactness are required, to form a right judgment, and to proportion the assent to the different evidence and probability of the thing; which rises and falls, according as those two foundations of credibility, viz. common observation in like cases, and particular testimonies in that particular instance, favour or contradict it. (Ibid., sec. 9)[4]

What I have called Hume's direct and reverse methods for establishing the evidential strength of testimony are precisely the same as Locke's "two foundations of credibility."

For reasons that will become evident, it will be useful to have a positive statement of the first—the direct—method for establishing the evidential force of testimony. We can do this by replacing testimonial weaknesses with testimonial strengths:

    1. The witnesses concur with one another, rather than contradict one another.

    2. The witnesses are many, not few.

    3. They are of unimpeachable, rather than of doubtful, character.

    4. They are disinterested, not interested, parties.

    5. They present their testimony in measured tones of confidence, rather than with hesitation or too violent asseveration.

To these marks of excellence we might add that these witnesses have special expertise relevant to the matter at hand; they are not gullible; they are not visually impaired; and so on. When criteria of this kind are satisfied, the evidence provided by the testimony increases, perhaps amounting to what Hume is willing to call a proof.

Similarly, the decision rendered through the use of the reverse method can also, according to Hume, amount to a proof. This occurs when the event attested to runs counter, in Locke's phrase, to "common observation in like cases." Common observation in like cases may provide a proof that events of a certain kind could not have taken place. So, just as unimpeachable testimony can supply strong support for the occurrence of an improbable event, the very high antecedent improbability of an event's occurring can supply strong support for asserting the nonoccurrence of that event. This sets the stage for the possibility of a clash of proof against proof—one a proof based on the direct method that an event did take place, the other a proof based on the reverse method that it did not. In such a circumstance, to repeat Locke's words, "diligence, attention, and exactness are required, to form a right judgment, and to proportion the assent to the different evidence and probability of the thing."

The dynamics of this conflict of proof against proof underlies the argumentative structure of Hume's treatment of miracles. Roughly, in part 1 Hume grants, for the sake of argument, that a circumstance could arise where testimony evaluated by the direct method amounts to a proof that a certain miraculous event has occurred, while, at the same time, the reverse method provides a proof that it could not have occurred. This contest between competing proofs is the organizing theme of part 1. Contrary to what many commentators seem to have thought, Hume does not attempt to settle this contest in part 1. Though Hume's tone leaves no doubt concerning how he thinks the contest will ultimately be settled, still, in part 1, no decision is officially declared—certainly not a tie. Stated broadly, the task of part 1 is to establish the appropriate standards for evaluating testimony in behalf of a miracle of *any kind*; the task of part 2 is to show that reports of *religious* mira-

cles have not in the past met these standards. Taking experience as his guide, Hume further concludes that there is no
likelihood that they will ever do so.

The reverse method for evaluating testimony. An important implication of the possibility of a conflict between the direct and the
reverse methods for evaluating testimony is that the evidential
force of testimony can vary with context. If a person we take to
be reliable tells us that a common sort of event has occurred,
trusting to his reliability, we usually accept his report without
hesitation. If, however, the very same person tells us that a perfectly fantastic event has occurred, we may then move in the
other direction and reconsider our belief in his reliability. Con-
versely, we may resist accepting reports of quite common events
if we take the person reporting them to be notoriously unreliable. It is in these ways, among others, that the evaluation of
testimony is deeply context-bound.

To see how these methods function in an ordinary, nonphilo-
sophical, context, consider a report from a "normally reliable
source" that President George W. Bush has been observed
walking a tightrope over his swimming pool. Most people's initial reaction would be justified disbelief. The sheer bizarreness
and improbability of such an event's taking place cast immediate doubt on the force of the testimony offered in its behalf. It
seems more reasonable to treat the report as a hoax or perhaps
as a misunderstanding of a political metaphor. This is a simple
and I believe uncontroversial example of the reverse method at
work. It might, in the event, turn out that Bush actually did
perform this feat, and did so before witnesses with video cam-
eras, and so on, putting it beyond doubt that he did so. (It's a
knack, he tells reporters, that he picked up as an undergraduate
at Yale.) In this case, the full satisfaction of the direct test of
testimony simply overrides the initially strong negative presumption generated against it by the reverse test.

We can next consider an example of a different kind, one that
will be useful later on. Though exaggerated, it has some basis in

fact. Henry—as we will call him—is full of stories about famous people he has met under unusual circumstances. Browsing in a bookstore in Greenwich Village, whom does he bump into but Woody Allen, thumbing through a collection of Baudelaire's poetry? They strike up a conversation that is continued over brunch at Balthazar. Flying to London, whom does he find sitting next to him? Bishop Desmond Tutu. There was the time he filled out a golf foursome including Michael Jordan. He was stuck in an elevator with Cindy Crawford. He fell in with Osama Bin Laden at (of all places) a disco in Beirut. The list of such remarkable meetings runs on and on, including encounters with Oprah Winfrey, Mother Teresa, Donald Trump, Stephen Hawking, Mikhail Baryshnikov, and each of the last three popes. For years Henry has enthralled (or bemused) dinner companions with stories of this kind.

What are we to think of Henry and his stories? If we look at them individually, and if we have no prior reason to distrust Henry, his stories may strike us as remarkable, but still believable. (No one of them is in a league with Bush's tightrope walking.) Many people have had chance encounters of this sort, and unless we have other reasons to distrust them, we are inclined to take their stories at face value. What seems highly implausible is that Henry could have been involved in all (or even most) of these encounters. As the list gets longer and longer, we move into the area of the utterly implausible and our opinion of the credibility of Henry's testimony correspondingly sinks. Invoking the reverse method, we will eventually conclude that the probability that all (or even most) of these stories are true is so low that we would not believe them even if they were told to us by Cato. As a result, we will not credit any single one of them if we have only Henry's word to go on.

We might, perhaps, wonder why Henry is retailing such stories. Perhaps he is delusional or a pathological liar or a prankster. Maybe he is putting what Hume called "natural principles of credulity" to an empirical test by seeing how far he can pull people's legs before they catch on. But however interesting these questions might be, they need not be answered for the reverse method to be decisive in rejecting the credibility of Henry's testimony. The sheer improbability that all (or most) of these things happened is sufficient for discounting his testimony, whatever his reasons for presenting it. There is, it is important to acknowledge, the remote possibility that Henry has told these stories because they happened just as he relates them. When we say, using the expression in the common way, that it is impossible that all (or even most) of these events took place, we are not assigning a probability of 0 to their joint occurrence—unless, that is, Henry slips and contradicts himself. (Henry, however, never makes slips of this kind.) We might investigate a suitably large, randomly selected sample of his stories and, much to our surprise, discover that, in all likelihood, all (or at least most) of Henry's stories are true. To put the matter differently, however strong our initial grounds for distrusting Henry's stories, provided that his stories are consistent, our distrust remains defeasible. This will be a matter of central importance later, in the examination of various (misguided) attacks on Hume's discussion of miracles.

This account of Henry and his stories is important for the following reason: it shows that the application of the reverse method depends upon the *improbability* that an event, or set of events could occur. In this case, the extreme improbability that troubles us arises through the joint assertion of events that, taken individually, are *not* sufficiently improbable to trouble us. Such an extreme improbability can arise in other ways as well. In the application of the reverse test of testimony, it is the extreme improbability, not its source, that matters.

We can make the transition to testimony concerning miracles by changing the Bush story in one respect: instead of being told that he tightrope-walked across his pool, we are told that he walked across the surface of the water. Surely we now have a story even more improbable than the original. But even if we have reached what we might consider a higher level of improbability, it would still be wrong to assign a probability of 0 to its occurrence. It is, however, a moral certainty—something amounting to a proof in Hume's use of this term—that no such event occurred. Given this, it would be perfectly reasonable to dismiss out of hand the testimony brought forward in its behalf.

To return to Henry for a moment. Although the probability that Henry met all the people he claims to have met is exceedingly low, it would not, except colloquially, be miraculous if he had done so. But a new step (or new plunge) is taken when we consider the case of someone's purportedly walking on water. We now seem to reach a new level of improbability. If we ask the question "Which is more improbable, that Henry met all the people he claims to have met or that Bush took a stroll across the surface of his pool?" most people, I believe, would unhesitatingly hold that the second is more improbable than the first. But if the reverse method is sufficient for dismissing Henry's testimony, it is hard to see how it cannot be *at least* as applicable to reports of miracles. There is certainly no reason for being *more* tolerant of testimony concerning miracles than we are of Henry's reports.[5]

The argument found in the text of part 1. The above examples are intended to illustrate the application of the reverse test of testimony—the test, as I hold, that underlies the argument of part 1 of Hume's discussion of miracles. The closing paragraphs of part 1 square exactly with this reading. I will quote them at length.

> But *in order to encrease the probability against the testimony of witnesses*, let us suppose, that the fact, which they affirm, instead of being only marvellous, is really miraculous; and suppose also, *that the testimony, considered apart and in itself, amounts to an entire proof*; in that case, there is proof against proof, of which the strongest must prevail, but still with a diminution of its force, in proportion to that of its antagonist.

A miracle is a violation of the laws of nature; and as a firm and unalterable experience has established these laws, the proof against a miracle, from the very nature of the fact, is as entire as any argument from experience can possibly be imagined. . . . *There must, therefore, be a uniform experience against every miraculous event, otherwise the event would not merit that appellation.* And as a uniform experience amounts to a proof, there is here a direct and full *proof*, from the nature of the fact, against the existence of any miracle; nor can such a proof be destroyed, or the miracle rendered credible, but by an opposite proof, which is superior.[6]

The plain consequence is (and it is a general maxim worthy of our attention), 'That *no testimony is sufficient to establish a miracle, unless the testimony be of such a kind, that its falsehood would be more miraculous, than the fact, which it endeavours to establish*: And even in that case, there is a mutual destruction of arguments, and the superior only gives us an assurance suitable to that degree of force, which remains, after deducting the inferior.' (*EHU*, 10.11–13, emphasis added)

The passage begins by speaking of another way of increasing "the probability against the testimony of witnesses." The increase occurs when we pass from considering testimony concerning the marvelous to testimony concerning the miraculous. To count as a miracle, the occurrence of an event must run counter to established natural laws—that is, laws backed by "a firm and unalterable experience." Given such experience, the occurrence of the event must appear very highly improbable. As Hume notes (and presumably defenders of miracles would agree on this), the occurrence of the event must seem highly improbable; "otherwise the event would not merit that appellation." The underlying point is this: if the reverse test can provide strong grounds for distrusting the reports of the marvelous, then, a fortiori, it can provide grounds at least as strong for distrusting reports of the miraculous. Beyond this, because laws of nature are backed by "a firm and unalterable experience," we are in possession of grounds amounting to a proof as "entire as any argument from experience can possibly be imagined" that the event in question could not have occurred.

Hume, however, does not end his argument with this claim. Notice that Hume here speaks of an "argument from *experience*"—that is, an argument, even if it amounts to a proof, that is capable of being threatened by a contrary proof. He asks us to imagine that such a threat occurs because "the testimony, considered apart and in itself, [also] amounts to an entire proof." When Hume speaks of the testimony that amounts to a proof when considered "apart and in itself," he is referring, it seems clear enough, to what I have called the *direct* method of evaluating testimony. We are, that is, supposed to assume that the witnesses to the supposed event consist of a sufficient number of reliable and disinterested judges, such that their testimony amounts to a proof (again in Hume's sense of a proof) that the event did occur. The upshot of granting this is that we are now faced with a proof confronting a contrary proof—one based on the reverse method, the other on the direct method. If such a situation could arise, who would win? It is tempting to think that Hume holds that the proof using the reverse method wins, or at least achieves a standoff. He does not say either of these things. Here is what he says instead: "If the falsehood of his testimony would be more miraculous, than the event which he relates; then, and not till then, can he pretend to command my belief or opinion" (*EHU*, 10.13). Namely, under the generous assumption that the testimony "apart and of itself" amounts to a proof, the defender of the occurrence of a miracle on the basis of such testimony still has a large mountain to scale. A proof on a par in strength with its counterproof yields no more than a draw. A direct proof stronger than the reverse counterproof will still be diminished in strength by the counterproof it surpasses. What is needed—to put it metaphorically—is a direct proof that outdistances the reverse counterproof by the full length of a proof. It seems, then, that on even the most generous assumption concerning the quality of the testimony relative to the direct standard, one who defends the existence of a miracle on the basis of such testimony is still faced with the formidable task of showing that the argument drawn from the internal quality of the testimony fully dominates the counterargument based on the empirically grounded improbability of the event's occurring.

It may, perhaps, seem strange for Hume to speak of two *entire* proofs coming into conflict with each other. This may even seem logically impossible. One way to avoid this difficulty is to say that Hume is merely speaking of two competing proofs that are *apparently* entire. In a sense this is correct, but Hume's way of speaking reflects our common understanding of what a proof is. Hume explains his use of the notion of a proof in a passage that occurs earlier in the *Enquiry*:

> Mr. LOCKE divides all arguments into demonstrative and probable. In this view, we must say, that it is only probable all men must die, or that the sun will rise to-morrow. But to conform our language more to common use, we ought to divide arguments into *demonstrations*, *proofs*, and *probabilities*. By *proofs* meaning such arguments from experience as leave no room for doubt or opposition. (*EHU*, 6 n. 10)

In this passage Hume speaks of conforming our language "to common use," and it is certainly true that in everyday language we do not restrict proofs to demonstrative arguments. A proof, commonly understood, is something that settles a matter— something that makes further investigation unnecessary, perhaps even irrational. For example, *A* can prove something to *B* by citing an appropriate reference work. Admittedly, as both *A* and *B* know, reference works sometimes contain errors, but in the common affairs of life that possibility is almost never *allowed* to count. Sometimes, however, we are forced to take such a possibility seriously—for example, when two respected reference works conflict. Here, if *A* had cited the second reference work instead of the first, that too would have counted as a proof.

When, however, the conflict between these sources becomes known, the situation changes in a radical way. If there is no good reason to give preference to one source over the other, they cancel each other out in just the way Hume suggests.

Elsewhere, I have employed the notion of *levels of scrutiny* to analyze situations of the kind just described.[7] Normally, citing an appropriate reference work settles a matter—no further examination or scrutiny of evidence is demanded. The situation changes, however, when, as in the above case, two reference works conflict. In this circumstance, the level of scrutiny rises and the reliability of the reference works themselves becomes an object of examination. From this new perspective we will not say that either citation amounts to a proof—though in the absence of such a conflict (or any other factor that triggers a higher level of scrutiny), each would have counted as a proof. It is just this kind of situation that Hume envisages when he speaks of a "proof against proof." The extreme improbability of a miraculous event's occurring by itself triggers a high level of scrutiny concerning the testimony brought forward in its behalf. This is how Hume's reverse method functions when applied to testimony in behalf of a miracle.

An argument not found in part 1. Consider the following argument:

1. A miracle is a violation of a law of nature.
2. A law of nature is an exceptionless (hence inviolate) regularity.

Therefore:

3. No miracles ever occur.

Because this argument cites no empirical evidence, we can call it the *a priori argument against the possibility of miracles*—or just the *a priori argument* for short. Hume never presents such an argument, but it is tempting to think, as I once did, that it or something like it lies in the background, doing the primary argumentative work.[8] I now think that this reading of the text is wholly mistaken. A number of considerations should put this beyond doubt.

It is not inconsequential that Hume nowhere explicitly formulates this argument, but some might think that he is so transparently committed to it that it is inconceivable that it does not play a guiding role in his thought. There are, however, two reasons that militate against this understanding of the text. First, if this really is his implicit background argument, it is hard to see why his *explicit* argument takes the form it does. As noted, Hume draws only a *conditional* conclusion at the close of part 1. How are we to explain this reticence if he believes himself in possession of a knockdown argument in favor of the unconditional rejection of miracles? Beyond this, the discussion of proofs confronting proofs—the central theme of part 1— would be out of place if a deeper argument existed that settled the issue straight off. Indeed, the entire discussion of testimony would appear otiose if it were possible to show, seemingly on a priori grounds, that no miracle has ever occurred, for then it would be a mere triviality that no testimony is ever sufficient to establish the occurrence of a miraculous event.

A second reason for rejecting the idea that Hume implicitly relies on such an a priori argument is that, in part 2, he explicitly rejects its conclusion by acknowledging that under certain circumstances it *could* be possible to establish the occurrence of a miracle on the basis of testimony. The miracle in question concerns a worldwide interlude of eight consecutive days of darkness. If Hume's treatment of miracles were grounded in the a priori argument to the effect that no miracle is ever possible, then granting this possibility would be an inexplicable lapse into incoherence. As we shall see, it is nothing of the kind.

I think Don Garrett says precisely the right thing concerning Hume's supposed reliance on an a priori argument against miracles:

> Hume is not arguing that the wise reject testimony for miracles because they recognize that miracles are impossible by definition. Nor is he claiming that no one could ever *observe* a miracle. He is

not missing the point by defining "miracle" in such a way that any event that actually occurs or is observed, no matter how bizarre, would fail to be a miracle. (Garrett 1997, 152)

To put it somewhat differently, Hume nowhere argues as follows: "Perhaps on some occasion a person did walk on water, but even so, it would still not be right to *call* it a miracle." As we shall see in examining the further development of Hume's argument as it unfolds in part 2, Hume's aim is not to achieve this shallow verbal victory—if it is a victory.

Is Hume's argument either circular or question-begging? From the start, Hume's treatment of miracles has been charged with being either circular or question-begging.[9] One of his eighteenth-century critics, William Samuel Powell, made this charge succinctly:

> But nature, we are told, is uniform and unvaried in her operations. This either presumes the point in question, or touches not those events which are supposed to be out of the course of nature. (Powell 1776, 95)

Some fifty years ago, C. S. Lewis offered essentially the same criticism in these words:

> Now of course we must agree with Hume that if there is absolutely "uniform experience" against miracles, if in other words they have never happened, why then they never have. Unfortunately we know the experience against them to be uniform only if we know that all reports of them are false. And we can know all the reports to be false only if we know already that miracles have never occurred. In fact, we are arguing in a circle. (Lewis 1947, 123)[10]

It takes only a few words to explain what is wrong with the circularity criticism. Hume nowhere argues, either explicitly or implicitly, that we know that all reports of miracles are false because we know that no such experiences have ever occurred. This almost gets the direction of Hume's argument backward.

Hume begins with a claim about testimony. On one side we have *wide* and *unproblematic* testimony to the effect that when people step into water they do not remain on its surface. On the other side we have isolated reports of people walking across the surface of water. Given testimony of the first kind, how are we to evaluate the testimony of the second sort? The testimony of the first sort does not show that the testimony of the second sort is false; it does, however, create a strong presumption—unless countered, a decisively strong presumption—in favor of its falsehood. That is Hume's argument, and there is nothing circular or question-begging about it. Those who think otherwise are in all likelihood working under the misapprehension that Hume's reasoning is being driven by an a priori argument against the very possibility of a miracle's occurring. If so, the mistake about circularity is being pushed from behind by the further mistake of attributing an a priori argument to Hume where there is none.

Of course, even if it is wrong to charge Hume with employing a question-begging argument against the possibility of miracles, he may still be wrong in his assessment of the credibility of at least some testimony that has been presented in their behalf. Making his case against the credibility of specifically religious miracles is the task of part 2.

The arguments of part 2. Part 2 opens with these words:

> In the foregoing reasoning we have supposed, that the testimony, upon which a miracle is founded, may possibly amount to an entire proof, and that the falsehood of that testimony would be a real prodigy: But it is easy to show, that we have been a great deal too liberal in our concession, and that there never was a miraculous event established on so full an evidence. (*EHU*, 10.14)

Hume backs this claim with four considerations. The first is that no testimony in behalf of miracles has ever passed what I have called the direct test. The passage is worth citing in full.

There is not to be found, in all history, any miracle attested by
a sufficient number of men, of such unquestioned good sense,
education, and learning, as to secure us against all delusion in
themselves; of such undoubted integrity, as to place them beyond
all suspicion of any design to deceive others; of such credit and
reputation in the eyes of mankind, as to have a great deal to lose
in case of their being detected in any falsehood; and at the same
time, attesting facts, performed in such a public manner, and in
so celebrated a part of the world, as to render the detection unavoidable: All which circumstances are requisite to give us a full
assurance in the testimony of men. (*EHU*, 10.15)[11]

Second, Hume offers a psychological account of the acceptance of reports of miracles, telling us that the "passion of *surprize* and *wonder*" (*EHU*, 10.16) arising from accounts of miracles can overpower our good sense.[12] In the third place he
remarks that accounts of miracles "are observed chiefly to
abound among ignorant and barbarous nations" (*EHU*, 10.20).
This seems like a special case of his first consideration, but
Hume singles it out for attention because it offers an explanation
of how beliefs in miraculous events gain their initial foothold.
Hume's fourth consideration demands close attention.

I may add as a *fourth* reason, which diminishes the authority of
prodigies, that there is no testimony for any, even those which
have not been expressly detected, that is not opposed by an infinite number of witnesses; so that not only the miracle destroys
the credit of the testimony, but the testimony destroys itself.
(*EHU*, 10.24)

Under this heading, Hume first notes that the miracles reported by different religions will stand in conflict with one another if they are intended, as they sometimes are, to establish
the *unique* legitimacy of one religion over all others. This is a
nice point, but I do not think it captures the full force of
Hume's fourth consideration. A deeper matter is introduced in
Hume's reflections on "a memorable story related by Cardinal

DE RETZ," where, without explicitly acknowledging that he is doing so, he reinvokes the reverse argument of part 1. The miracle in question was supposed to have taken place in Saragossa, the capital of Aragon. It was reported that a doorkeeper at the city's cathedral had his missing leg restored by the application of holy oil to the stump. This miracle was attested to by a large number of supposedly reliable witnesses. Even so, Cardinal De Retz would have none of it. Hume praises the sagacity and good sense of the cardinal in these words:

> [Cardinal DE Retz] considered justly, that it was not requisite, in order to reject a fact of this nature, to be able accurately to disprove the testimony, and to trace its falsehood, through all the circumstances of knavery and credulity which produced it. . . . He therefore concluded, like a just reasoner, that such an evidence carried falsehood upon the very face of it, and that a miracle, supported by any human testimony, was more properly a subject of derision than of argument. (*EHU*, 10.26)

In a similar vein, Hume dismisses the numerous miraculous cures attributed to the Jansenist abbé of Paris. In doing so, however, he seems to express himself in ways that run counter to the interpretation I am giving of his argument. Here is what he says:

> There surely never was a greater number of miracles ascribed to one person, than those, which were lately said to have been wrought in FRANCE upon the tomb of Abbé PARIS, the famous JANSENIST, with whose sanctity the people were so long deluded. The curing of the sick, giving hearing to the deaf, and sight to the blind, were every where talked of as the usual effects of that holy sepulchre. But what is more extraordinary; many of the miracles were immediately proved upon the spot, before judges of unquestioned integrity, attested by witnesses of credit and distinction, in a learned age, and on the most eminent theatre that is now in the world. Nor is this all: A relation of them was published and dispersed every where; nor were the JESUITS, though a learned

body, supported by the civil magistrate, and determined enemies to those opinions, in whose favour the miracles were said to have been wrought, ever able distinctly to refute or detect them. Where shall we find such a number of circumstances, agreeing to the corroboration of one fact? (*EHU*, 10.27)

In this passage, Hume seems to concede, without qualification, that the testimony in behalf of these miracles amounted to full proofs. He continues:

And what have we to oppose to such a cloud of witnesses, but the absolute impossibility or miraculous nature of the events, which they relate? And this surely, in the eyes of all reasonable people, will alone be regarded as a sufficient refutation. (*EHU*, 10.27)

Here it plainly seems that we have testimony amounting to a proof on one side being overridden by some kind of a priori argument on the other. This is precisely the argument that I claim Hume does not employ.

We need only consider Hume's further remarks about this "cloud of witnesses" to see that he does not put the debate on this footing:

Is the consequence just, because some human testimony has the utmost force and authority in some cases, when it relates the battle of PHILIPPI or PHARSALIA for instance; that therefore all kinds of testimony must, in all cases, have equal force and authority? (*EHU*, 10.28)

Hume then goes on to undermine the testimony concerning the abbé's miraculous gifts:

How many stories of this nature have, in all ages, been detected and exploded in their infancy? How many more have been celebrated for a time, and have afterwards sunk into neglect and oblivion? Where such reports, therefore, fly about, the solution of the phenomenon is obvious; and we judge in conformity to regular experience and observation, when we account for it by the known and natural principles of credulity and delusion. And shall we, rather than have a recourse to so natural a solution, allow of a miraculous violation of the most established laws of nature? (*EHU*, 10.31)

We then get the ringing conclusion:

Upon the whole, then, it appears, that no testimony for any kind of miracle has ever amounted to a probability, much less to a proof; and that, even supposing it amounted to a proof, it would be opposed by another proof; derived from the very nature of the fact, which it would endeavour to establish. It is experience only, which gives authority to human testimony; and it is the same experience, which assures us of the laws of nature. When, therefore, these two kinds of experience are contrary, we have nothing to do but subtract the one from the other, and embrace an opinion, either on one side or the other, with that assurance which arises from the remainder. But according to the principle here explained, this subtraction, with regard to all popular religions, amounts to an entire annihilation; and therefore we may establish it as a maxim, that no human testimony can have such force as to prove a miracle, and make it a just foundation for any such system of religion. (*EHU*, 10.35)

It seems, then, that what started as an apparent problem for my reading of the text ends up confirming it.[13]

A limitation on the scope of the argument. In the passage just cited, Hume claims to have established as a maxim "that no human testimony can have such force as to prove a miracle, and make it a just foundation for any such system of religion." The phrasing here is important. As stated, it does not completely rule out the possibility of testimony establishing the occurrence of a miracle, for Hume's maxim is limited in its scope to miracles intended to serve as the foundation for a system of religion. Hume underscores this point.

I beg the limitations here made may be remarked, when I say, that a miracle can never be proved, so as to be the foundation of a system of religion. For I own, that otherwise, there may possibly be miracles, or violations of the usual course of nature, of such a kind as to admit of proof from human testimony; though, perhaps, it will be impossible to find any such in all the records of history. Thus, suppose, all authors, in all languages, agree, that, from the first of JANUARY 1600, there was a total darkness over the whole earth for eight days: Suppose that the tradition of this extraordinary event is still strong and lively among the people: That all travellers, who return from foreign countries, bring us accounts of the same tradition, without the least variation or contradiction: It is evident, that our present philosophers, instead of doubting the fact, ought to receive it as certain, and ought to search for the causes whence it might be derived. The decay, corruption, and dissolution of nature, is an event rendered probable by so many analogies, that any phenomenon, which seems to have a tendency towards that catastrophe, comes within the reach of human testimony, if that testimony be very extensive and uniform. (*EHU*, 10.36)

This passage, though often neglected and usually treated as problematic when not neglected, is of crucial importance. First, it shows—if this still needs showing—that Hume's argument concerning miracles is not an a priori argument in character. For example, it is not an argument intended to show that the notion of a miracle as a violation of a law of nature is somehow self-defeating or logically impossible. Second, and more importantly, it shows that the contest between the direct method and the reverse method of evaluating testimony in support of a miraculous event need not always favor the reverse method. For notice the care that Hume has taken in tailoring his example of eight days of total darkness to satisfy the demands of the direct method of evaluating testimony laid out above. In the case as he describes it, there will be testimony from "a sufficient number of men, of such unquestioned good sense, education, and learning, as to secure us against all delusion in themselves." As the example states, all such men will attest to the occurrence of this event. We may also assume that a great many of these witnesses to the event are of sufficient integrity to foreclose any question of deceit. In any case, the event reported was open to all to observe, and an attempt at deceit could hardly have gone undetected. Because it was a worldwide phenomenon, the original reports of such an event would not be limited to "ignorant and barbarous nations." Finally, as described, there are no religious motives involved that might raise suspicions on that score. Against all these direct reasons for taking the testimony to be reliable, we have only the countervailing force of the reverse reason against it based on the improbability that well-established laws of nature have been violated.[14] In such a circumstance (if one were ever to occur), Hume here acknowledges that the testimony may fully outweigh the reverse argument based upon the improbability of the event.

This passage may also help us understand what Hume has in mind when he speaks of a law of nature. In the present context Hume cannot be treating a law of nature as an invariant regularity in nature, for if he did so, the occurrence of a miracle (including the miracle of eight days of darkness) could be ruled out on definitional grounds alone, and, given this, all of Hume's talk about testimony would be idle. Garrett has suggested that we should model our understanding of a law of nature on a "subjective" reading of Hume's second definition of a cause:

> In Treatise I.iii.14, and again in Enquiry VII, Hume offers two different definitions of the term "cause," the first in terms of constant conjunction of resembling events, and the second in terms of association and inference in the mind. Not only the term "cause" but also such related terms as "proof," hence also "law of nature" and "miracle," are susceptible to the same kind of subjective/absolute ambiguity in Hume. In the context of "Of Miracles," however, it is clear from the structure of the argument that Hume is appealing to *subjective* senses of "proof," "laws of nature," and

"miracle". For if a law of nature were understood as a completely uniform constant conjunction . . . the very notion of an exception to a law of nature would be contradictory. (Garrett 1997, 152)

Garrett's suggestion is both textually well grounded and systematically motivated, and I think it likely that, deep down, it is the right thing to say. Here I am inclined to deal with this matter in a much simpler way. The expression "law of nature" is commonly used in two different—though systematically related—ways: sometimes as a label for uniform regularity in nature, at other times as a *statement of* or *belief in* such a regularity. The following encyclopedia entry employs both of these uses in a single sentence:

> The basic law of current flow is Ohm's law, discovered by German physicist Georg Ohm, stating that the amount of current is directly proportional to the electromotive force and inversely proportional to the total resistance of the circuit. (Microsoft *Encarta*)

When we speak of a law's being discovered, we have in mind a regularity or functional relationship that exists in nature—something there to be discovered. When we speak of a law's stating something, we then have in mind a formulation of the law, something commonly called a principle. The notion of a law taken the first way indicates an invariance in nature; the notion of a law taken in the second way indicates an unqualified commitment to a proposition stating this invariance. Both ways of speaking are legitimate and, in a given context, are usually implicitly understood. Hume himself speaks in both ways.[15] However, when Hume tells us that "a firm and unalterable experience has established these laws," he can be speaking only about laws in a propositional sense. Experience confirms the principle formulated in Ohm's law; it does not arrange the world such that electrical currents obey it. The wise reasoner is guided by principles carrying this high level of confirmation, and for this reason she takes herself to be justified in rejecting reports of events that go against those principles, *unless*, that is, the evidence in favor of the events dominates the evidence in favor of the law. In such a conflict we have evidence facing evidence, and the matter can be resolved only through the weighing of evidence. This is precisely the situation Hume envisages when evaluating testimony in behalf of a miracle. Hume's example of eight days of darkness is intended to show that, given the right sort of testimony, the balance can shift, and principles with strong backing from past experience can be dominated by reliable evidence presenting counterinstances to them.

Here a new question arises. If Hume acknowledges that, under certain circumstances at least, the occurrence of a miracle could be established by testimony, how can he defend himself against the charge of mere prejudice in treating testimony in behalf of *religious* miracles with special disfavor? The Reverend William Warburton, one of Hume's most vigorous contemporary critics, put the matter this way:

> His spite, we see, is not against miracles, but only against the workers of them; for why, I pray you, are we to make this distinction? Are not the two facts equally attested by the concurrent evidence of all concerned? Are they not equally miraculous? for the absence of the sun eight days together from the globe of the earth is surely as *contrary* to the common course of nature as the resurrection of one from the dead. If he believes that, from the beginning, none ever rose from the dead, he believes, too, that there never was a total darkness for eight days together. Here, then, the *uniform experience*, as he calls it, is, in both cases, the same; yet we must believe the one, and not the other. Here spoke the true sense, as well as spirit, of modern infidelity;—we must reject *that* miracle, for whose working, by the interposition of God, we *can* give a reasonable account, and embrace that for which there is *no account to be given at all*. (Warburton 1841, 313)

As if anticipating a criticism of this kind, Hume counters it with a straightforward statement of fact:

> Should [a] miracle be ascribed to any new system of religion; men, in all ages, have been so much imposed on by ridiculous stories

of that kind, that this very circumstance would be a full proof of a cheat, and sufficient, with all men of sense, not only to make them reject the fact, but even reject it without farther examination. . . . As the violations of truth are more common in the testimony concerning religious miracles, than in that concerning any other matter of fact; this must diminish very much the authority of the former testimony, and make us form a general resolution, never to lend any attention to it, with whatever specious pretence it may be covered. (*EHU*, 10.38)

In short, for Hume, it is an empirical fact, amply illustrated by history, that testimony concerning religious miracles is notoriously unreliable. On the basis of this general fact about the quality of such testimony, the wise reasoner has ample grounds for rejecting it.

This does not mean that on a priori grounds no amount of testimony could ever establish the occurrence of a religious miracle. To alter Hume's own example, suppose that for eight days all was dark save for an illuminated face that simultaneously appeared throughout the world, speaking in a way intelligible to all, offering many proofs of his or her magnificence, and so on. (The story could be further filled in with universal cures, resurrections, whatever.) We would then have a case that does parallel Hume's example of a natural miracle, and it would surely be a matter of prejudice for him to reject the testimony in behalf of the religious miracle while accepting the testimony in behalf of the natural miracle. Hume's point, however, is that the local, sect-serving testimony that has been offered in behalf of religious miracles falls hopelessly short of standards of testimony satisfied by Hume's imagined case of a natural miracle. Warburton simply missed the point of Hume's example of the eight days of total darkness. He was not the last to do so.

Was part 1 even necessary? It is often held, or at least tacitly assumed, that Hume's examination of miracles in the *Enquiry* falls into two distinct parts, each intended to be sufficient in its own way in showing that testimony has never been adequate for establishing the occurrence of a miracle. This, I have argued, is simply wrong. The argument of part 1 presents no unconditional conclusion concerning the status of testimony in behalf of miracles. Its task is to lay down standards that, given the character of a miracle, any such testimony must meet. It does not foreclose the possibility that these standards could be met. It certainly throws up no a priori barriers in the way of doing so. Hume's argument concerning miracles—specifically concerning religious miracles—is completed only in the second part of the essay, where he argues, *as a matter of fact*, that such testimony has never come close to meeting these standards. This is not something he simply appends to the argument in part 1; it is an essential step toward his conclusion that "a miracle can never be proved, so as to be the foundation of a system of religion."

But now a reverse problem may seem to arise. If, in the end, Hume's attack on the legitimacy of testimony in favor of religious miracles depends on the assessment of probabilities, why did he present the argument of part 1 at all? The question itself may embody a misunderstanding of the character of the argument of part 1, namely, that it is purely conceptual, hence a priori in character. That, I have argued, is a mistake. The reverse argument of part 1 is also a probabilistic argument intended to call into question the adequacy of testimony put forward in behalf of miraculous events. Part 1 invokes the principle that the extreme improbability of an event's occurring itself provides grounds for calling into question the legitimacy of the testimony presented in its behalf. When the occurrence of the event is highly improbable, the standards of scrutiny rise and the challenge becomes correspondingly more forceful. Given this principle, we are *entitled* to apply very high (ultrahigh) standards to the testimony intended to establish the occurrence of a miracle. This is a key move, because it shows that Hume is not simply being arbitrary or prejudiced in insisting that the standards appropriate for evaluating testimony in behalf of miracles are much higher than the standards we normally apply in evaluating testimony.

Yet even if the standards for testimony in behalf of miracles are high, they remain, in principle, satisfiable. That is the point of Hume's example of the eight days of total darkness. The example shows what it would be like to meet such high standards. In contrast, those who cite testimony in support of religious miracles seem to have no understanding of what the appropriate standards should be. Thus, properly understood, the two parts of Hume's discussion of miracles operate in tandem. Through probabilistic reasoning, part 1 fixes the appropriate level of scrutiny for evaluating testimony with respect to miracles; part 2 considers the quality of the testimony that has hitherto been brought forth in support of religious miracles and concludes that it comes nowhere near to meeting the appropriate standards. More strongly, an examination of historical records shows such a consistent pattern of ignorance, deceit, and credulity that the wise reasoner is fully justified in rejecting all testimony given in support of a miracle intended to serve as the foundation of a system of religion.

2

Two Recent Critics

IN OFFERING THE ABOVE account of Hume's treatment of miracles, I have not considered recent criticisms that have been brought against it. It seemed better to give a full exposition of his position before turning to this matter. In the last few years there has been a spate of attacks—"bashes" might be a better word—aimed at Hume's treatment of miracles. Here I will examine two representative examples: David Johnson's *Hume, Holism, and Miracles* and John Earman's *Hume's Abject Failure: The Argument against Miracles*. What I say in response to their criticisms can, I think, be used to reply to criticisms presented by others.

At the beginning of this essay I remarked that, to understand Hume's position, one must avoid a number of mistakes of interpretation. One mistake is to suppose that Hume thinks the argument of part 1 is adequate *in itself* to show "that no testimony is sufficient to establish a miracle" (*EHU*, 10.13). A second mistake, which is often tied to the first, is to attribute to Hume an a priori argument against the possibility of a miracle or an a priori argument against the possibility that testimony can establish the occurrence of a miracle—specifically, an argument that turns on the conceptual relationships among *laws of nature*, *violations of laws of nature*, and *miracles*. We can call critics of Hume who make either or both of these mistakes *gross misreaders* of the text. Gross misreadings of this kind almost always carry with them a wholly unfounded criticism, namely, that Hume's argument is circular—perhaps transparently or risibly so. It is, however, possible to develop criticisms of Hume's arguments that do not depend on such gross misreadings. A more subtle strategy involves arguing that Hume's treatment of miracles rests on presuppositions or commitments that are themselves unacceptable. This maneuver can include a dismissal of the shallow criticisms of Hume that have been produced by the gross misreaders. Tendentiously, I will call critics of this second kind *subtle misreaders* of Hume. Johnson will serve as our specimen of a gross misreader, Earman as our specimen of a subtle misreader. I will examine Johnson's work first.

Here is Johnson's general assessment of Hume's treatment of miracles:

> The view that there is in Hume's essay, or in what can be reconstructed from it, any argument or reply or objection that is even superficially good, much less, powerful or devastating, is simply a philosophical myth. The mostly willing hearers who have been swayed by Hume on this matter have been held captive by nothing other than Hume's great eloquence. (Johnson 1999, 4)

Johnson's broad strategy in attempting to support this assessment is to argue along the following lines: Hume's argument, as it appears in the text, is *transparently* question-begging, so it must either be rejected out of hand or be given a charitable reconstruction that makes it immune to this charge. It turns out, however, that all such reconstructions encounter dilemmas of their own: either the defect of question-begging reappears at a deeper level or the proof becomes so attenuated that Hume's original conclusion is not established.

Here I will confine myself to Johnson's treatment of Hume's own argument, setting aside Johnson's analyses and criticisms of various "reconstructions." Citing Richard Swinburne with apparent approval, Johnson describes the task of part 1 of

Hume's treatment of miracles as follows:

> The burden of the first part is that of, as Richard Swinburne has
> put it, "showing on philosophical grounds that the evidence
> against the occurrence of any purported miracle is normally likely
> to be extremely strong and to outweigh by far the evidence in
> favor of the occurrence." (Ibid., 2)

Clearly, if what I have said above is correct, this characterization
of part 1 as having a self-contained argument concerning miracles is simply false. As we have seen, Hume draws no unconditional conclusion about the strength of evidence for or against
the occurrence of miracles at the close of part 1. His rhetoric
certainly indicates the conclusion he is heading toward, but
Hume recognizes the need to deliver the evidential goods before drawing a summary conclusion.

Setting aside his patronizing tone, Johnson does better in
characterizing the role of part 2.

> The burden of the second part of Hume's essay is that of showing,
> mostly on supposed historical and psychohistorical grounds, that
> the evidence in favor of such miracles as have actually been alleged
> to occur is extremely weak indeed. (Ibid.)

That is correct, but what is missing here is a recognition of
the systematic connection between the two parts of Hume's
discussion. It is not surprising that, having severed this connection, Johnson tells us that he will "focus on the argument of the
first part of Hume's essay" and then "explain why [he] think[s]
that these philosophical grounds are entirely specious" (ibid.).
Johnson could, of course, point out that he is not the only one
who has taken part 1 as a self-contained philosophical argument—many of Hume's supporters share this view. This may,
indeed, be the majority view. If the textual analysis offered
above is correct, then the majority view is just wrong.

Suppose, however, we go along with Johnson's self-contained
view of part 1. How well, under this assumption, does he do?

Not very. As Johnson acknowledges, the crucial component in his attack turns on his understanding of what Hume means by a proof as it occurs in the expression "proof against proof." In the *Enquiry* Hume actually says little about how he understands the notion of a proof. In a footnote cited earlier, we saw that Hume amends Locke's twofold classification of arguments into demonstrations and probabilities, saying "to conform our language more to common use, we ought to divide arguments into *demonstrations*, *proofs*, and *probabilities*. By *proofs* meaning such arguments from experience as leave no room for doubt or opposition." In this passage Hume does not deny that there is a sharp division between arguments that are demonstrative and those that are not; he simply comments, quite rightly, that it sounds odd to *speak* of probabilities when the evidence cited leaves no practical room for doubt. As noted above, a proof taken in this sense is not in principle immune to future refutation, as sound demonstrative arguments are, but, in certain contexts where the evidence is simply overwhelming, it would be idle, perhaps even irresponsible, to be concerned about this possibility. This reflects one way that the notion of a proof is commonly understood and is, as explained above, how Hume understands this notion.

Johnson's criticism of Hume depends on giving the notion of a proof a much stronger interpretation. He relies on the following passage:

> A wise man, therefore, proportions his belief to the evidence. In such conclusions as are founded on an infallible experience, he expects the event with the last degree of assurance, and regards his past experience as a full *proof* of the future existence of that event. In other cases, he proceeds with more caution: He weighs the opposite experiments: He considers which side is supported by the greater number of experiments: To that side he inclines, with doubt and hesitation; and when at last he fixes his judgment, the evidence exceeds not what we properly call *probability*. All probability, then, supposes an opposition of experiments and ob-

servations; where the one side is found to overbalance the other, and to produce a degree of evidence, proportioned to the superiority. (*EHU*, 10.4)

On the basis of this passage, Johnson offers the following syntactically convoluted account of Hume's notion of a proof:

> For present purposes, all we need is the abundantly clear fact that Hume holds that every *nonstatistical inductive inference* we make— every inference we make of the form *all hitherto observed* (examined, relevantly tested, etc.) A*s are B*s*, hence all A*s are B*s*, where *we know that the inductive premise is true*—is a "proof," and vice versa. (Johnson 1999, 12)

The "and vice versa" that ends this passage attributes to Hume the view that being a proper nonstatistical inductive inference is not only a sufficient condition, but also a necessary condition, for being a proof. For Hume, Johnson is saying, all proper nonstatistical inductive inferences are proofs and, rather more surprisingly, all proofs are proper nonstatistical inductive inferences.

Having given this strong specification of what Hume means (or perhaps must mean) by a proof, Johnson turns to Hume's temporary concession that the testimony in behalf of a miracle also "amounts to" a proof.

> We have *in favor* of the miracle, I suppose, since in this first part of the essay Hume is supposing that the testimony may "amount to" a proof, the conjunction of the following two items, of which only the latter is a *proof* as such:
>
> (i) Some witness of type A says that he observed the miracle occur.
>
> (ii) All hitherto observed (that is, tested for accuracy) witnesses of type A are completely accurate reporters.
>
> Hence: All witnesses of type A are completely accurate reporters. (Ibid., 17)

This, then, is how Johnson understands Hume's notion of a competition of proof against proof: On one side we have a proof based on an established *natural law* that rules out the possibility that a miraculous event *E* could occur. On the other side we have another *natural law* establishing the reliability of the kind of testimony presented in behalf of the occurrence of some miracle. If that reading were correct, then Hume would be committed to the view that the battle of proof against proof would inevitably yield an exact, irremediable standoff. This, however, is not Hume's position. As we have seen, Hume ends part 1 with a conditional conclusion that leaves open the possibility that further evidence may shift the balance in favor of one supposed proof over the other. In part 2 Hume then argues that the uniformly tainted quality of the testimony brought forward in behalf of religious miracles decisively shifts the balance to favor the evidence that the miracle did not occur. With respect to a report of a nonreligious miracle (for example, eight days of worldwide darkness), Hume acknowledges that the balance could shift in the reverse direction. None of this makes sense on Johnson's understanding of what Hume meant by a proof.

Oddly, having gone to the trouble of characterizing what he takes to be Hume's understanding of the clash of proof against proof, Johnson simply drops the subject of competing nonstatistical inductions and falls back on the standard charge that Hume's argument is question-begging:

> Hume apparently begs the question. The issue on the table is whether we should believe a witness who claims to have observed a miracle, an *A* that is not a *B*. Hume, I have suggested, assumes that . . . we have against the miracle a proof, so that in particular we have a known inductive premiss, describing "a uniform experience," to the effect that all hitherto *A*s are *B*s. But the question of whether we know so general an inductive premiss is essentially the same as the question of whether we know that the *A* observed by the witness was a *B*, or (as the witness claims) not a *B*. (Ibid., 18)

This, however, simply misrepresents the situation. We are not dealing with a clash of experience against experience. We are involved in assessing the credentials of testimony in behalf of a type of event that runs deeply counter to common experience.

No assumption is made to the effect that the supposed witnesses did not have the experience they reported having, so no question is begged. I have said this already, but it seems worth repeating in response to an egregious (and more than a little haughty) offender.

To backtrack. In stating his criticism of Hume, Johnson tells us that "Hume apparently begs the question." Here the word "apparently" may sound cautious, perhaps even generous. That is not Johnson's intention. His point is that Hume's writing is so obscure that it may not be possible to determine what sort of argument he is presenting and therefore not possible to charge him definitively with producing a question-begging argument. As he tells us, "It seems . . . that Hume's own argument either obviously begs the question, or becomes obscure" (ibid., 21).

Seemingly in an effort to exhibit this obscurity, Johnson suggests that Hume, "at least in some moods," actually relies on what we have called the a priori argument.

> Hume might, and in at least some moods certainly would, protest that he is not just *assuming* that we have a proof, and hence "a uniform experience," against a given miracle, but that this follows from the very fact that the alleged event is a miracle. "There must . . . be a uniform experience against every miraculous event, otherwise the event would not merit that appellation." But if this is the claim, then, *first*, Hume is saying that it is a necessary truth that every miracle is opposed by a uniform experience ("where [I presume for now] the past has been entirely regular and uniform")—that there *must* be a uniform experience against *every* miraculous event—which is difficult to reconcile with what he says about the imaginary but possible *miracle* of the eight days of darkness. (Ibid., 19)

This is all wildly out of focus. What the example of eight days of darkness was explicitly intended to show is that there is nothing inherently impossible about a miraculous event's occurring and nothing inherently impossible about testimony's establishing that it did occur. Hume goes to some pains to describe how the occurrence of a miracle, if one were to occur, could be established. This, as we have seen, plainly implies that Hume in *none* of his moods is relying on a purely a priori argument of this kind.

One last point. The enemies of Hume's treatment of miracles are often—though not always—friends of miracles themselves. Friends of miracles face a task similar to Hume's, namely, to give an account of miracles that, on one hand, does not exclude their occurrence on a priori grounds yet, on the other hand, preserves their miraculous character. Here is Johnson's attempt to provide such a definition:

> I will say, then, that for any person x, for any time t, for any possible event m, m is a *miracle* for x at t if and only if m actually occurs at some time and m is a violation of (an exception to) something which is for x at t exceedingly well established, relative to a body of inductive evidence, as being a law of nature. (This, of course, does not imply that a miracle for x at t must *occur at t*.) More pithily, I will say that *a miracle is a violation of an apparent law of nature*, where the indexing to person and time, and the epistemic aspect above, is built into the word "apparent." (Ibid., 9)

Johnson provides little commentary on what seems to be a weak, highly relativized, epistemic definition of a miracle. A miracle of this kind may not be substantial enough to be worth considering. But I will waive this point. Given this definition, Johnson issues a challenge to the defender of Hume.

> We seek, then, Hume's (or a Humean) argument for at least the weaker than usual version of Hume's conclusion (of the first part of his essay) mentioned in the preceding chapter, which we now state in the following way:

> (H) Where m is a possible event, allegedly actual and allegedly witnessed, and where L is (for us, now) an apparent law, which any actual occurrence of m would have violated, and where (thus) L is (for us, now) exceedingly well established,

relative to a body of inductive evidence, as being a law of
nature, then, at the very least, the testimony of *one* human
witness (not identical to any of us) who claims to have observed *m*'s occurrence can never rightly convince us that
m has occurred—the testimony of *one* such supposed witness to *m*'s occurrence will always be "outweighed" by the
inductive evidence which so strongly supports *L*. (Ibid.,
9–10)

Clearly what Johnson is demanding is some form of an a priori
argument to be found in part 1 that establishes this conclusion.
The answer is that Hume makes no effort to meet this demand,
and it is a gross misunderstanding to think that he either intended to or had to.

We move into a new realm when we turn to John Earman's
Hume's Abject Failure: The Argument against Miracles. For some
time I accepted what I took to be a well-grounded empirical
generalization that, going back to the eighteenth century, critics of Hume's treatment of miracles have uniformly misread the
text in a gross way. Earman's work provides a clear counterex-
ample to this claim. He not only avoids what I have called the
gross misreading of the text; he explicitly rejects it. I will show
this shortly, but first there is an unpleasant matter to get out of
the way.

For reasons that escape me, Earman often seems as much
concerned with attacking Hume's reputation as with criticizing
Hume's argument. Here is his opening statement:

Section X ("Of Miracles") of Hume's *Enquiry Concerning Human
Understanding* is a failure. In philosophy, where almost all ambi-
tious projects are failures, this may seem a mild criticism. So to
be blunt, I contend that "Of Miracles" is an abject failure. It is
not simply that Hume's essay does not achieve its goals, but that
his goals are ambiguous and confused. Most of Hume's considerations are unoriginal, warmed over versions of arguments that are

found in the writings of predecessors and contemporaries. And the parts of "Of Miracles" that set Hume apart do not stand up to scrutiny. Worse still, the essay reveals the weakness and the poverty of Hume's own account of induction and probabilistic reasoning. And to cap it all off, the essay represents the kind of overreaching that gives philosophy a bad name. (Earman 2000, 3)

Here is his summary conclusion:

> While the essay will endure as an important historical artifact and as a signpost to interesting philosophical issues, those philoso-phers who try to mine it for nuggets of wisdom are bound to be disappointed—it is a confection of rhetoric and *schein Geld*. (Ibid., 73)

In between, Earman beats an endless tattoo of such invective. For whatever reason, he seems to think it important not only to refute Hume's argument, but also to display Hume's head on a pike. When Hume received similar hard treatment in George Campbell's *Dissertation of Miracles*, he responded to Hugh Blair, who had sent him a copy of this work, in these words:

> I could wish that your friend had not chosen to appear as a contro-versial writer, but had endeavoured to establish his principles in general, without any reference to a particular book or person; tho I own he does me a great deal of honour, in thinking that any thing I have wrote deserves his attention. For besides many incon-veniences, which attend that kind of writing, I see it is almost impossible to preserve decency and good manners in it. This au-thor, for instance, says sometimes obliging things of me much beyond what I can presume to deserve; and I thence conclude that in general he did not mean to insult me: yet I meet with some other passages more worthy of Warburton and his followers than of so ingenious an author. (Hume 1932, letter 188)[16]

That said, Hume proceeds to respond to Campbell's criticisms. Following Hume's example, I will set aside Earman's rhetorical excess and concentrate on three philosophically relevant questions: *How does Earman understand Hume's position? What is his substantive criticism of it?* and *Is his criticism any good?*

As already noted, Earman identifies and rejects what I have called the gross misreading of the text. First, he does not assert or assume that Hume intended to produce a complete, self-contained argument in part 1.

> Hume does not say explicitly [at the close of part 1] that what is left after the clash of proofs is never sufficient to ground the credibility of a miracle, and, indeed, he nowhere explicitly states [an argument to that effect]. Nor is it plausible that [this] is what Hume thought, even if it is not what he explicitly says. For one thing, this reading would make it hard to understand the function of the famous Maxim which Hume enunciates at the close of Part 1. . . . For another thing, Part 2 would be puzzling since there Hume allows that especially good testimony can establish the credibility of some secular miracles. Thus, I will assume . . . that in Part 1 Hume did not mean to foreclose the issue of whether testimony could establish the credibility of a miracle, although I acknowledge that the text is ambiguous enough to allow [this] reading. (Earman 2000, 21–22).[17]

Second, Earman also dismisses (or at least seems to dismiss) the claim that Hume's argument is purely definitional in character:

> Admirers of Hume never tire of trying to saddle miracle enthusiasts with a dilemma stemming from the very definition of "miracle." Although there are many versions of the dilemma, I have yet to find one that can rightly be attributed to Hume and, at the same time, has any real force. (Ibid., 14)

This passage is peculiarly worded, for, as stated, it leaves open two possibilities: (1) that Hume's text does contain a version of the definitional argument, but one that has no force, or (2) that there is a version of the definitional argument that has force but does not occur in Hume's text. We can assume that Earman does not embrace the second possibility, and nothing in his reading of Hume suggests that he embraces the first. It seems reasonable to assume, then, that Earman does not attribute this definitional argument to Hume. In the third place, Earman nowhere repeats the standard charge of begging the question. In sum, Earman seems to be free of the mistakes that make up what I have called the gross misreading of the text. Among Hume's critics, this makes Earman perhaps unique.

What then are Earman's grounds for calling Hume's treatment of miracles a failure, indeed, an abject failure? As far as I can see, abuse aside, Earman's criticism turns on a single point. It depends fully on Earman's account of what Hume understands by an inductive argument amounting to a proof. I will quote the central passages at some length.

> To understand the structure of Hume's argument, it is helpful to try to specify the form that Hume thinks inductive reasoning follows. As a starting point, recall Reichenbach's *straight rule of induction*: If n As have been examined and m have been found to be Bs, then the probability that the next A examined will be a B is m/n. Corollary: If m = n, then the probability that the next A will be a B is 1. Hume also thought that induction proceeds by a straight rule which is not easy to formulate in general but which takes on a simple form in the case of uniform experience. As a first cut, we can try to state the corollary as: If n As have been examined, all of which were found to be Bs, then if n is sufficiently large, the probability that all As are Bs is 1. How large "sufficiently large" needs to be is presumably a matter to be settled by psychological investigations. (Ibid., 22–23)

Having attributed a simple version of the straight rule to Hume, Earman goes on to attribute the following argument to him as well.

> So here in a nutshell is Hume's first argument against miracles. A (Hume) miracle is a violation of a presumptive law of nature. By Hume's straight rule of induction, experience confers a probability of 1 on a presumptive law. Hence, the probability of a miracle is flatly zero. Very simple. And very crude. (Ibid., 23)

Let me say at once that if Earman is correct in attributing this argument to Hume, then Hume's case is hopeless. The hopelessness is generated by a consideration that I will attempt to explain informally. Suppose some body of evidence E bestows a probability of 1 on some hypothesis H. This is usually formulated as $Pr\ (H/E) = 1$. Now suppose that we gather some further evidence A (some of which may bear against H); adding this further evidence to E can never lower the probability below 1. Symbolically:

If $Pr\ (H/E) = 1$ then $Pr\ (H/E \& A) = 1$

It is not generally true that acquiring additional evidence will leave a prior probability assignment unchanged. To take a simple example: by asking, we discover that almost all of the students in the first three rows of a class are in-state students. This seems to provide a reasonable basis for the hypothesis that most of the students in the classroom are in-state students. We then discover to our surprise that the next three rows contain mainly out-of-state students. We then adjust our probability assignment downward to accommodate this new fact. How this is done in detail can be complicated, but here we need only make the simple point: When the conditional probability of a hypothesis lies between the extremes of 1 and 0, additional evidence can lead us to revise the probability assignment either up or down. When, however, it lies at either of the extreme points, additional evidence cannot budge it. At these endpoints, conditional probability of the hypothesis is unrevisable or indefeasible (monotonic) in the light of further evidence.

It is easy to see how the crude version of the straight rule that Earman attributes to Hume, combined with the above theorem of conditional probability, leads to disaster. In a section entitled "Hume's Stultification of Scientific Inquiry," Earman provides the following example of the unwanted dogmatism generated by these joint commitments:

Among the zillions of protons observed by particle physicists, none has been verified to decay. But particle physicists do not assign a probability of 1 to the proposition that the next proton to be observed will not decay, and they certainly do not think that they have adequate inductive grounds for probabilistic certainty with respect to the general proposition that no proton ever decays—otherwise the expenditure of time and money on experiments to detect proton decay would be inexplicable on the standard expected utility model of decision making. (Ibid., 31)

This is certainly correct, and if Hume's inductive principles lead to a result contrary to it, I am willing to acknowledge that Earman has made his case against Hume. Whether he has done so will depend on two considerations. First, and most importantly, is Earman correct in attributing to Hume what he calls "Hume's straight rule"? Second, is he correct in saying that Hume's argument concerning miracles depends on the use of this straight rule? I think that the answer to both questions is no.

What is Earman's evidence in support of attributing Hume's straight rule to Hume? As far as I can see, it depends wholly on the occurrence of a number of strongly stated conclusions. He cites several instances of such strong talk. Some of them sound very strong indeed. Here is one example found in a letter of 1761 written to Hugh Blair:

The proof against a miracle, as it is founded on invariable experience, is a *species* or *kind* which is full and certain when taken alone, because it implies no doubt, as is the case with all probabilities. (Hume 1932, letter 350)

This specimen of strong talk may seem to settle the matter, but it doesn't. Earlier we noted how Hume understands the distinction between proof and probability:

To conform our language more to common use, we ought to divide arguments into *demonstrations*, *proofs*, and *probabilities*. By *proofs* meaning such arguments from experience as leave no room for doubt or opposition. (*EHU*, 6 n. 10)

Here, as earlier suggested, I think it is important to take seriously the expression "to conform our language more to common use." Taken quite literally, it concerns the way we speak. Hume, it seems, is correct about this, for when we speak of probabilities we suggest—or conversationally imply—that some genuine, though perhaps small, doubt remains. By using strong language, we cancel this conversational implication. We all do this—even, my guess is, Earman during his off-hours. That we talk in this way does not commit us to anything like Hume's straight rule.

To put the matter somewhat differently, although it is a mistake to cite Hume's strong talk as the basis for attributing to him a commitment to the straight rule of induction, it would not be off the mark to say that sufficiently rich evidence could lead someone to speak and act *as if* or to speak and act *almost as if* a probability assignment of 1 (or 0) to a hypothesis is justified. When the evidence is strong enough to make something a moral certainty, then a concern with further evidence ceases. This, I think, is the appropriate interpretation of Cardinal De Retz's behavior. Rightly or wrongly, given (what he takes to be) his wide knowledge of religious fakery and the credulity of those deceived by it, De Retz thinks that it is not worth his trouble to examine the credentials of the local miracle reported to him. (We can imagine him being interrupted by a servant who reports the miracle of the restored leg, shrugging and responding, "Oh, not another miracle; will they never cease?") Someone who, speaking technically, assigns a probability of 0 to the hypothesis that this miracle had taken place would talk and act in the same way. There is, however, this difference. Cardinal De Retz's moral certainty, though robust, remains defeasible. It would take a great deal to budge De Retz from his skepticism, but it still remains possible that he could be budged. In sum, it is not enough to cite various instances of strongly stated conclusions as the basis for saddling Hume with what Earman tendentiously calls "Hume's straight rule." The matter has to be settled at a level deeper than this.

The most obvious place to look for Hume's own views on probability is in the three successive chapters in part 3 of book 1 of the *Treatise of Human Nature* entitled

11. Of the probability of chances
12. Of the probability of causes
13. Of unphilosophical probability

These sections raise serious problems of interpretation, for Hume sometimes seems to slide back and forth between two activities: offering something like an analysis of probability judgments, and giving a causal account of how such judgments are formed. Hume seems to slide back and forth between a descriptive and a normative standpoint. It can also be hard to take seriously (or at least literally) Hume's account of the way in which probabilities are determined by the dispersion of a limited quantity of vivacity over the available options. Yet, even faced with these difficulties, these three sections are primary texts for our understanding of his general position concerning probability. For whatever reason, Earman largely ignores them.

If Earman had turned to them, he would have encountered a position that, though mathematically naive, is broadly Bayesian in character.[18] These sections indicate that Hume comes close to meeting Earman's own criteria for being a Bayesian.[19] First, Hume is clearly committed to the notion of degrees of belief. Second, arguably his perhaps quaint account of the dispersion of a finite stock of vivacity (the source of belief) over available alternatives is presented in a way that yields the standard axioms of probability theory.[20] More significantly, he seems to hold that "rational degrees of belief should be regimented according to the probability calculus" (Earman 2000, 26). This is borne out in section 13 where, in a remarkable anticipation of the works of Daniel Kahneman and Amos Tver-

sky,[21] Hume examines the errors that arise when partial beliefs
are formed under the influence of exogenous or improperly
weighed factors. So far, so Bayesian—at least in general orienta-
tion. Hume is mum about the appropriate procedures for up-
dating probability assessments in response to new evidence.
Even so, there is no sign in this context—the context where
Hume offers his most detailed account of probability—that
Hume is committed to the straight rule Earman attributes to
him.

More deeply, the attribution of such a straight rule to Hume
seems to be flatly incompatible with one of Hume's most fundamental claims, namely, that the "course of nature may
change."[22] This assertion lies at the heart of Hume's skeptical
argument concerning induction. The pithiest statement of that
argument occurs in the *Abstract of the Treatise*:

> What is possible can never be demonstrated to be false; and 'tis
> possible the course of nature may change, since we can conceive
> such a change. Nay, I will go farther, and assert, that he could not
> so much as prove by any *probable* arguments, that the future must
> be conformable to the past. (*THN, Abstract*, 14)

Hume goes on to introduce his circularity argument, intended
to show that any attempt to prove that the course of nature
cannot change would be circular. But that argument, whether
it is correct or not, is not our present concern. What is of interest here is that his belief that the course of nature may change
seems to carry the immediate consequence (for him) that no
inductive generalization (except one involving a complete enu-
meration) is unrevisable, is indefeasible, or has a conditional
probability of 1. This is compatible with saying that, with sufficiently strong evidence, we may think and act as if the conditional probability on our evidence is 1. We may even be hard-
wired to do so. But an uneliminable fallibilism lies at the heart
of Hume's philosophy, and that on its face precludes attributing
"Hume's straight rule" to him.

Finally, it would settle the issue decisively if we could find texts where Hume actually speaks of something like a full proof's being open to revision. There are at least two such examples. The first occurs in a portion of the *Treatise* that is usually ignored and when not ignored usually ridiculed: section 1 of part 4 of book 1, entitled "Scepticism with Regard to Reason." I have no interest in defending the argument or even explicating it in depth;[23] I cite it only as a dramatic example of Hume's willingness to revise downward judgments of the highest degree of warrant. Here is the opening passage of this section:

> In all demonstrative sciences the rules are certain and infallible; but when we apply them, our fallible and uncertain faculties are very apt to depart from them, and fall into error. We must, therefore, in every reasoning form a new judgment, as a check or controul on our first judgment or belief; and must enlarge our view to comprehend a kind of history of all the instances, wherein our understanding has deceiv'd us, compar'd with those, wherein its testimony was just and true. Our reason must be consider'd as a kind of cause, of which truth is the natural effect; but such-a-one as, by the irruption of other causes, and by the inconstancy of our mental powers, may frequently be prevented. By this means all knowledge degenerates into probability; and this probability is greater or less, according to our experience of the veracity or deceitfulness of our understanding, and according to the simplicity or intricacy of the question. (*THN*, 1.4.1.1)

Having shown to his satisfaction how knowledge "degenerates" in this manner into probability, he next applies the same style of reasoning to probability itself, telling us that "in every judgment, which we can form concerning probability, as well as concerning knowledge, we ought always to correct the first judgment, deriv'd from the nature of the object, by another judgment, deriv'd from the nature of the understanding" (*THN*, 1.4.1.5). Hume then recursively applies this method to

successively nested probability judgments and arrives at the following conclusion:

> Having thus found in every probability, beside the original uncer-
> tainty inherent in the subject, a new uncertainty deriv'd from the
> weakness of that faculty, which judges, and having adjusted these
> two together, we are oblig'd by our reason to add a new doubt,
> deriv'd from the possibility of error in the estimation we make
> of the truth and fidelity of our faculties. This is a doubt, which
> immediately occurs to us, and of which, if we wou'd closely pursue
> our reason, we cannot avoid giving a decision. But this decision,
> tho' it shou'd be favourable to our preceding judgment, being
> founded only on probability, must weaken still farther our first
> evidence, and must itself be weaken'd by a fourth doubt of the
> same kind, and so on *in infinitum*; till at last there remain nothing
> of the original probability, however great we may suppose it to
> have been, and however small the diminution by every new uncer-
> tainty. (*THN*, 1.4.1.6)

I am not suggesting that this is a good argument, though it is
not altogether easy to say what is wrong with it. The point is
that this is not an argument that someone committed to what
Earman calls Hume's straight rule would produce.

I said that there are two Humean texts that plainly show that
Hume does not accept Hume's straight rule. The second text
is the section on miracles itself; Earman half acknowledges this.
Earlier I remarked that two questions should be distinguished:
Was Hume committed to Hume's straight rule? And *Does Hume
rely on the straight rule in his treatment of miracles?* These questions are not unrelated. If Hume uses Hume's straight rule in
his treatment of miracles, then, at least there, he is committed
to it. So does he or doesn't he? Earman is rather shifty on this
matter. At first he seems to attribute precisely such an argument
to Hume. I'll repeat it:

> So here in a nutshell is Hume's first argument against miracles.
> A (Hume) miracle is a violation of a presumptive law of nature.

> By Hume's straight rule of induction, experience confers a proba-
> bility of 1 on a presumptive law. Hence, the probability of a mira-
> cle is flatly zero. Very simple. And very crude. (Earman 2000, 23)

Eight pages later Earman returns to this question and speaks in a much more reserved way. He asks whether Hume actually intended to adopt a view that implied that the probability of a presumptive law is 1, hence unrevisable. In other words, he asks whether Hume actually adopted Hume's straight rule in order to reject the possibility of a miracle.

> Is this a result that Hume intended? Strictly speaking, the ques-
> tion is meaningless since Hume does not explicitly use the lan-
> guage of conditional probability. Nevertheless, there is both posi-
> tive and negative evidence about whether Hume intended a
> consequence like this one. (Ibid., 31)

In defense of ascribing the straight rule to Hume, Earman cites Hume's remark that Cardinal De Retz was a "just rea-soner" in concluding that the evidence for the restoration of the amputated leg "carried falsehood on the very face of it, and that a miracle supported by any human testimony was more properly a subject of derision than of argument."[24] I have al-ready argued that the use of such strong language does not, by itself, show that Hume accepted and employed Hume's straight rule. Admittedly, the language here is very strong, but the con-text in which it occurs is plainly concerned with religious mira-cles, and with respect to those sorts of miracles Hume holds that it is a moral evidential certainty that the miracle did not occur. A reliance on Hume's straight rule does not have to come into it at all.

On the negative side, Earman explicitly concedes that the attribution of Hume's straight rule to Hume runs dead counter to the stated text concerning miracles.

> When uniform experience supports a law statement L that is con-
> tradicted by testimony, Hume speaks of putting "proof against

proof, of which the strongest must prevail, but still with a diminution of its force, in proportion to that of its antagonist" (*E* 114;
143). This idea is reiterated in the letter to Blair quoted above in
section 9. After claiming to provide a proof against miracles that
"implies no doubt," he adds: "[B]ut there are degrees of this species [of proof], and when a weaker proof is opposed to a stronger,
it is overcome" (*L*, Vol. I, 350). But if the weighing of proof
against proof is to be done within the ambit of the probability
calculus and the rule of conditionalization, then Hume's straight
rule has to be dropped—his proof in favor of L by uniform experience cannot be taken to mean probability 1 but at most a high
probability that is short of 1. Consequently, uniform experience
does *not* furnish a proof against a miracle in the sense of making
the conditional probability of its occurrence flatly zero, although
this probability may be very, very tiny. (Ibid., 32)

Doesn't this concession simply undercut Earman's basic interpretation of Hume's argument, and with it undercut his criticism of it? Earman's response to the worry is peculiar indeed:

Such a concession is far from tiny since it would mean that the
distinction between a (Hume) miracle and a marvel is a matter of
degree rather than of kind. And once the concession is granted,
it is natural to wonder how it can be that testimonial evidence can
ground belief in marvels but not in (Hume) miracles. (Ibid.)

First, Earman makes it sound as though Hume is conceding
something, whereas, in fact, Earman is conceding that his fundamental interpretive claim runs counter to a central theme of
the text. Second, and perhaps stranger still, his wonder concerning "how it can be that testimonial evidence can ground
belief in marvels but not in (Hume) miracles"[25] is completely
misplaced because, as Earman recognizes, in part 2 Hume explicitly says that under certain highly constraining circumstances testimony can ground belief in a miracle.[26]

What can be said in summary about Earman's attempt to
show that Hume's argument against miracles is an abject fail-

ure? If we set aside his attacks on Hume's reputation, his originality, and what might be the misguided enthusiasm of some
of Hume's admirers—which, after all, are hardly to the point—
Earman's criticism turns on a single claim: Hume's argument,
he holds, depends on a commitment to what Earman calls
Hume's straight rule, and that rule has disastrous conse-
quences. The evidence he cites in favor of this attribution is
Hume's frequent use of strong conclusionary language. I have
argued that his speaking in this common sort of way does not
warrant our assigning to Hume a commitment to an unpalat-
able version of the straight rule. On the other side, we have the
fact, which Earman acknowledges, that the attribution of such
a rule of induction runs counter to the general structure of
Hume's essay on miracles and, beyond this, at certain key
points is explicitly at odds with the text. To this, I would add
(and have tried to show) that such an attribution runs counter
to a central feature of Hume's philosophical standpoint: his
fallibilism. Is Earman's argument against Hume's treatment of
miracles, then, a failure? I think it is. Is it an abject failure? It
is enough to say it is a failure.

3

The Place of "Of Miracles" in Hume's Philosophy

THE INTERPRETATION of a philosophical text is often a controversial matter, with commentators disagreeing even about the basic aspects of the work under consideration. Clearly I read Hume's discussion of miracles in ways that are radically different from the readings offered by Johnson and Earman. Are there principles or guidelines that we can appeal to in trying to decide how a philosophical text should be interpreted? In the introduction to *Philosophical Interpretations*—a collection of articles in which I offer analyses of texts by Wittgenstein, Hume, Berkeley, Plato, and others—I suggest two such principles. The first is the principle of *local interpretation*: "To understand the point of a philosophical remark or philosophical argument, we must ask what the remark or argument is intended to do in just the context in which it appears. Precisely how does it move the enterprise along?" (Fogelin 1992, 6). Complementing this principle is another, which I call the principle of *global interpretation*. It tells us to place the particular remark (together with the context that immediately surrounds it) in the broader context of the philosophical position as a whole and perhaps, beyond this, in the historical context in which the position itself emerged (ibid.). The first is a principle of close reading; the second is a principle of broad understanding. Both principles strike me as platitudes, but, like many platitudes, they are often ignored. David Johnson, it seems to me, consistently violates both principles. He misreads the text of "Of Miracles," and his general understanding of Hume's position hardly reaches past part 1 of the essay. John Earman is better at getting the text of section 10 right, but he goes wrong by attributing to Hume views that are not found in the text of that section. Beyond this, he attributes to Hume doctrines that are actually incompatible with central claims that Hume makes elsewhere in his writings. I am referring, of course, to his attribution of "Hume's straight rule" to Hume.

Thus far in this work, I have largely been guided by the principle of local interpretation, staying close to the text of section 10. In closing I will present some reflections from the second—global—perspective. Our question is this: How does Hume's discussion of miracles relate to the fundamental features of his philosophical standpoint? The answer is that Hume's attitude toward miracles is of a piece with some of his most fundamental philosophical commitments.

Hume's philosophical position has various levels, dimensions, and themes, and it is a subtle and complex challenge to understand how these components fit together to form a coherent whole. Different styles of interpreting Hume's philosophy usually turn on how these various aspects of his position are weighted and assembled. I will not attempt to produce such a synoptic view here, but will simply enumerate central themes in Hume's philosophy and then ask how his treatment of miracles is related to them.

  1. To begin with, Hume was committed to an empiricist account of the origin and nature of ideas. All complex ideas are reducible to simple ideas, and all simple ideas derive from simple impressions that they resemble.
  2. Hume's philosophy had a strong skeptical component, including a skepticism concerning our knowledge of

the external world and, more famously, a skepticism concerning inductive inferences.

3. Hume held that an idea has the status of a belief (rather than, say, a supposition), not in virtue of a distinctive content, but in virtue of possessing a certain liveliness or vivacity. The vivacity found in ideas that makes them beliefs can be traced back to the vivacity inherent in impressions.

4. Hume's central task, as he saw it, was to discover, as far as possible, the underlying causal principles that account for the behavior of human beings and human institutions.

5. Hume offered an account of causal relations that either identified them with a certain kind of constant conjunction or at least held that such a constant conjunction was one of their central features. He further held that the existence of a causal relation could be established only by an appeal to experience, and thus could not be established by a priori reasoning alone.

This is all too schematic, but perhaps it is enough to situate Hume's treatment of miracles within his general philosophical position.[27]

The first component, which we might call the official empiricist component, plays no direct role in Hume's treatment of miracles. At no place are we invited to seek out the impression or system of impressions corresponding to some idea. The discussion does not take place at that level. It may be possible to trace a route back from the discussion of miracles to these underlying empiricist principles, but the connection is not argumentatively close. It is not, for example, enough to point to supposed weaknesses in Hume's treatment of impressions and ideas as grounds for dismissing whatever it is he has to say about miracles. Hume's commitments concerning impressions and ideas do not have the status of *premises* for his conclusions concerning the evidential status of miracles.

Similar remarks hold for the second component, Hume's commitment to, or at least use of, strong skeptical arguments. Once more there is a difference in level. Hume's skeptical arguments are offered, as he tells us, *in support* of his theory of the fixation of causal beliefs.

> My intention then in displaying so carefully the arguments of that fantastic sect, is only to make the reader sensible of the truth of my hypothesis, *that all our reasonings concerning causes and effects, are deriv'd from nothing but custom; and that belief is more properly an act of the sensitive, than of the cogitative part of our natures.* (*THN*, 1.4.1.8)

This passage comes from a section of the *Treatise* titled "Of scepticism with regard to reason," but the claim he is making holds quite generally for his employment of large-scale skeptical arguments: their target is always the pretensions of reason or the pretensions of philosophical positions that rely too heavily on reason. Hume, to my knowledge, never makes the mistake of employing a general skeptical argument to secure an advantage for a special theory when that special theory is equally subject to skeptical attack. As noted, Hume nowhere bases his assessment of testimony in behalf of miracles on a general skepticism concerning testimony itself.

The third component of Hume's position, his theory that ideas amount to beliefs in virtue of their liveliness or vivacity, makes a cameo appearance in his discussion of miracles when he tells us, "The passion of *surprize* and *wonder*, arising from miracles, being an agreeable emotion, gives a sensible tendency towards the belief of those events, from which it is derived" (*EHU*, 10.16). We have also noted that Hume, in both the *Treatise* and the *Enquiry*, bases his own "subjective" account of probability on this theory of belief. In his treatment of miracles, it is, however, the probabilistic argument that matters, not Hume's background theory concerning the nature of probabilistic reasoning. The former could be sound even if the latter were rejected. The important point to make here, pace John Earman's claims, is that neither in the text of "Of Miracles" nor in Hume's background theory of probabilistic reasoning do we find a commitment to a naive straight rule of inductive inference.

The fourth component, which concerns Hume's broad commitment to a naturalistic program for the behavioral sciences, bears directly on the theoretical motivations for Hume's treatment of miracles. In the subtitle of the *Treatise*, Hume describes his project as an "attempt to introduce the experimental method of reasoning into moral subjects." By this he signals his intention to model his approach to what he called the "science of man" (what we now call the behavioral and social sciences) using methods analogous to those employed in the physical sciences. If we look to Newtonian physics for our model of a science, we find, at least for the most part, an empirical enterprise intended to discover the causal laws governing the physical world. This is certainly how Hume viewed Newton's achievements. Setting aside the question whether Hume is always true to this ideal, we see Hume presenting himself as engaged in an empirical investigation intended to discover the causal laws governing human actions and human institutions. Hume's ambition, as is often said, was to become the Newton of the mind.

There is, however, an obvious barrier to this program: If there are no (or few) causal regularities governing human behavior or human institutions, then there is nothing (or little) for Hume's "science of man" to discover. The existence of *free will*—or liberty, as Hume prefers to call it—seems to present one such barrier to giving accounts of human behavior purely in terms of antecedent causal conditions. Hume is aware of this challenge and responds to it in both the *Treatise* and the *Enquiry* in sections titled "Of Liberty and Necessity." I wish to look briefly at this discussion because it has, I think, a theoretical motivation similar to that of Hume's treatment of miracles.

The examination of liberty is considerably different in these two works. In the *Treatise*, Hume, for the most part, identifies liberty with chance and then dismisses it as a fantastical idea. Here is Hume's closing brief against the possibility of liberty or free will:

> According to my definitions, necessity makes an essential part of causation; and consequently liberty, by removing necessity, removes also causes, and is the very same thing with chance. As chance is commonly thought to imply a contradiction, and is at least directly contrary to experience, there are always the same arguments against liberty or free-will. (*THN*, 2.3.1.18)

In the *Enquiry*, Hume adopts a different strategy in dealing with the supposed threat of liberty to his construction of a science of human behavior. In the *Treatise*, he held, as many have, that liberty is incompatible with causal necessity, and, for this reason, denied the existence of liberty. In the *Enquiry*, Hume changed his mind, arguing that liberty, properly understood, is compatible with the causal necessitation of human actions. He put the matter this way: "All men have ever agreed in the doctrine both of necessity and of liberty, according to any reasonable sense, which can be put on these terms; and that the whole controversy has hitherto turned merely upon words" (*EHU*, 8.3). To simplify his discussion: Hume's key idea is that the opposite of liberty is constraint, not necessity, whereas the opposite of necessity is chance, not liberty. Therefore, there need be no conflict between liberty and necessity.

Because Hume's compatibilist views concerning liberty and necessity are of considerable interest in their own right, they have attracted a great deal of attention. For present purposes, however, it is more important to note that, whatever their differences in the treatment of liberty, both the *Treatise* and the *Enquiry* are unequivocal in their commitment to a deterministic view of human behavior. This passage from the *Enquiry* is as strong as any found in the *Treatise*:

> The same motives always produce the same actions: The same events follow from the same causes. Ambition, avarice, self-love,

vanity, friendship, generosity, public spirit; these passions, mixed in various degrees, and distributed through society, have been, from the beginning of the world, and still are, the source of all the actions and enterprizes, which have ever been observed among mankind. . . . Mankind are so much the same, in all times and places, that history informs us of nothing new or strange in this particular. (*EHU*, 8.7)[28]

In an ingenious passage Hume illustrates the parity of causality in the physical and social realms by noticing how seamlessly they can blend.

And indeed, when we consider how aptly *natural* and *moral* evidence link together, and form only one chain of argument, we shall make no scruple to allow, that they are of the same nature, and derived from the same principles. A prisoner, who has neither money nor interest, discovers the impossibility of his escape, as well when he considers the obstinacy of the gaoler, as the walls and bars, with which he is surrounded; and, in all attempts for his freedom, chooses rather to work upon the stone and iron of the one, than upon the inflexible nature of the other. The same prisoner, when conducted to the scaffold, foresees his death as certainly from the constancy and fidelity of his guards, as from the operation of the ax or wheel. (*EHU*, 8.19)

This is almost a verbatim repetition of a passage found in the *Treatise* (*THN*, 2.3.1.17). It is, I take it, clear why Hume insists on the determinacy or regularity of human behavior: If there were choices that were genuinely spontaneous—that is, unpredictable on the basis of antecedent causal conditions—then, with respect to such choices, Hume's proposed "science of man" could have nothing to say. If these spontaneous actions were widespread or occurred in key contexts, there would be little prospect of developing a successful science of human nature at all.

Hume's deepest commitment to determinism is found in his rejection of the view that beliefs can be formed by spontaneous acts of the mind. For Hume, beliefs are also determined by antecedent causal conditions. Not only our external behavior, but also the inner workings of our minds, are part of the natural causal order. Because Hume adopts a version of a desire/belief account of human actions—that is, the view that human actions are the product of desires together with beliefs concerning how they can be fulfilled—a commitment to determinism at this level is essential to his entire enterprise of developing a science of human behavior.

Turning now to miracles: Without denying that Hume's general loathing for religious enthusiasm affected the tone of his writing on miracles, it is, I think, important to see his treatment of miracles as of a piece with his general commitment to the methods of natural science. Any event or activity whose causes lie outside the natural order represents a limitation on natural science. That itself, for Hume, creates a presumption against it. Furthermore, miracles have a long history of being connected with significant political events. Historically, sovereigns are often pictured as gaining their power and legitimacy from a divine grant or through divine inspiration. To the extent that such miraculous interventions are acknowledged, history and the science of politics could not be pursued in the naturalistic spirit that Hume adopts.[29] Neither miracles nor spontaneous free acts have a place in Hume's naturalistic worldview. This is an important reason why he is hostile to both.

Concerning the fifth component of Hume's position, he not only set himself the task of giving causal accounts of human behavior; he did so under the constraints of a particular understanding of the nature of causal relations. He held that causal laws involve regularities among events. For Hume, whether something exists or not (including whether an event has occurred or not) is something that can be settled only by an appeal to experience. From this it follows that causal regularities can be established only through an appeal to experience. This is one of Hume's most fundamental commitments.

With respect to miracles, Hume's strategy is to use the canons of causal reasoning to evaluate testimony brought forward in their behalf. Because, for him, no matter of fact can be established a priori, it remains an open, though remote, possibility that testimony could establish the occurrence of a miracle. That is the point of the discussion of eight days of darkness. With respect to miracles intended to serve as the foundation of a religion, the situation, according to Hume, is *factually* different. When we examine the testimony brought forward in their behalf, we see that it has *uniformly* failed to meet appropriate standards of acceptability. This uniform unreliability provides us with a proof—not a demonstration—that testimony offered in behalf of religious miracles cannot be trusted. If testimony in behalf of a religious miracle were found that could meet the appropriately high standards for acceptance, then Hume's proof would be overthrown. So, in the end, Hume's case against the acceptance of testimony in support of religious miracles turns on an assessment of factual evidence. Is his argument then merely a posteriori? The word "merely" is out of place. Given Hume's fundamental commitments, it could not take any other form.

Appendix I

Hume's Curious Relationship to Tillotson

HUME OPENS HIS EXAMINATION of the testimony in behalf of miracles with these words:

> THERE is, in Dr. TILLOTSON's writings, an argument against the *real presence*, which is as concise, and elegant, and strong as any argument can possibly be supposed against a doctrine, so little worthy of a serious refutation. (*EHU*, 10.1)

After sketching what he presents as Tillotson's basic argument against the doctrine of the real presence (or transubstantiation), Hume tells his reader:

> I flatter myself, that I have discovered an argument of a like nature, which, if just, will, with the wise and learned, be an everlasting check to all kinds of superstitious delusion, and consequently, will be useful as long as the world endures. For so long, I presume, will the accounts of miracles and prodigies be found in all history, sacred and profane. (*EHU*, 10.2)

These remarks suggest that Tillotson's argument against transubstantiation will provide an interpretive guide to understanding Hume's treatment of miracles. How, then, does Hume understand Tillotson's argument against transubstantiation? Here is what Hume says:

> It is acknowledged on all hands, says that learned prelate, that the authority, either of the scripture or of tradition, is founded merely in the testimony of the apostles, who were eye-witnesses to those

miracles of our Saviour, by which he proved his divine mission. Our evidence, then, for the truth of the CHRISTIAN religion is less than the evidence for the truth of our senses; because, even in the first authors of our religion, it was no greater; and it is evident it must diminish in passing from them to their disciples; nor can any one rest such confidence in their testimony, as in the immediate object of his senses. But a weaker evidence can never destroy a stronger; and therefore, were the doctrine of the real presence ever so clearly revealed in scripture, it were directly contrary to the rules of just reasoning to give our assent to it. (*EHU*, 10.1)

Tillotson would not be pleased with any of this. In the first place, as a number of writers have noted, the argument that Hume attributes to Tillotson cannot be found in Tillotson's writings.[30] Specifically, a key component in the argument that Hume attributes to Tillotson is the claim that evidence in behalf of transubstantiation must "diminish in passing from [the first authors of our religion] to their disciples." Nowhere in the relevant texts does Tillotson employ this *diminution* argument, as we might call it. Indeed, as we shall see, Tillotson would reject it as running dead counter to his central reason for rejecting the doctrine of transubstantiation. For that matter, Hume, in his treatment of miracles, does not employ this diminution argument either and, in fact, specifically rejects a variation of it in the *Treatise*.[31] So what exactly is going on? In an attempt to answer this, we can look more closely at what Tillotson actually does say in his polemic against the doctrine of transubstantiation.

Hume does not identify the texts he has in mind in acknowledging his debt to Tillotson. There are two obvious candidates: Sermon 11, "The Hazard of being Sav'd in the Church of *Rome*," and Sermon 26, "Discourse against Transubstantiation" (Tillotson 1742, 77–84, 190–203). In "The Hazard of being Sav'd in the Church of *Rome*," the doctrine of transubstantiation is listed as one of five dogmas of Roman Catholicism that make it difficult, though, as Tillotson concedes, not *strictly* impossible, for a Roman Catholic to achieve salvation. (The other four dogmas are the doctrine of infallibility, the doctrine of repentance, the doctrine of purgatory, and the doctrine of deposing kings in case of heresy.) The "Discourse against Transubstantiation" is an extensive elaboration of the argument found in the earlier Sermon 11.

Both sermons exhibit the same argumentative structure. Because it is more thorough—as well as more diverting—I will consider the argument presented in Sermon 26.

Tillotson offers various kinds of objections to the doctrine of transubstantiation. Some are scriptural. He argues that there is no need to take Christ's words "This is my body" literally rather than figuratively. To this end, he cites a long series of passages from the Gospels that can only, with good sense, be taken figuratively. For example, on a purely literal reading of the texts, we would be committed to saying that Christ was a *door*, a *vine*, and his church, again literally, *his body*. About such "Expressions in Scripture," Tillotson tells us, "every Man understands in a figurative, and not in a strictly literal and absurd sense" (ibid., 192). Tillotson also treats transubstantiation as a form of idolatry, dismissing it as equivalent to the barbaric doctrine that a god has been made so "that we may eat him" (ibid., 202). Hume would, I think, take pleasure in these sallies, but they cannot be the texts he has in mind when he speaks of Tillotson's "concise" and "elegant" argument, which his own argument concerning miracles is like in nature.

The closest we get to an argument of the sort Hume attributed to Tillotson, in broad outline, goes as follows: Let us suppose that the doctrine of transubstantiation is true. The thing we take to be bread is not bread but "the body of a man." Let us further suppose that the thing we take to be wine is not wine but is blood instead. In that case, our eyes would be deceiving us in a most extraordinary way—so extraordinary that, as reasonable people, we should give up all reliance on them. If, however, we were to do this, we would also have to reject the eyewitness reports of miracles "wrought by our Savior and his apostles, the assurances whereof did at first depend upon the certainty of sense" (ibid., 203). Most strikingly, this skepticism with regard to the senses would destroy the credibility of the apostles' reports of Christ's appearing to them after his resurrection. In a most remarkable passage, Tillotson imagines the apostles challenging the risen Christ in these words:

> Lord, it is but a few days ago since thou didst teach us not to believe our senses, but directly contrary to what we saw, *viz.* that the Bread which thou gavest us in the Sacrament, though we saw it and handled it and tasted it to be Bread, yet was not Bread, but thine own natural Body; and now thou appealest to our senses, to

prove that this is thy body which we now see. If seeing and han-
dling be an unquestionable Evidence that things are what they
appear to our senses, then we were deceived before in the Sacrament; and if they be not, then we are not sure now that this is thy
Body which we now see and handle, but it may be perhaps Bread
under the appearance of Flesh and Bones; just as in the Sacrament, that which we saw and handled and tasted to be Bread, was
thy Flesh and Bones under the form and appearance of Bread.
(Ibid.)

In short, Tillotson argues that the doctrine of transubstantiation leads
to a general skepticism in regard to the senses, which in turn undercuts
the testimony in behalf of those miracles that serve as the foundation
of the Christian religion. As he puts it, "never were any two things so
ill coupled together as the doctrine of Christianity and that of transubstantiation" (ibid.). Whether this is a good argument or a bad one, it
is certainly different from the argument attributed to Tillotson by
Hume. It is not similar to Hume's argument either.

There is, however, one place in Sermon 26 where the phrasing in
Tillotson's discussion of transubstantiation bears some similarity to
Hume's phrasing in his treatment of miracles. According to Tillotson
the doctrine of transubstantiation, if taken up as a dogma of Christianity, would itself have to be certified by a miracle. This, Tillotson tells
us, would prove a self-defeating enterprise:

For that there is a Miracle wrought to prove *that what* [one] *sees
in the Sacrament is not Bread but the Body of Christ*, there is only the
evidence of sense; and there is the very same Evidence to prove
that what [one] *sees in the Sacrament is not the Body of Christ but
Bread.* . . . And then the Argument for *Transubstantiation* and the
Objection against it would just balance one another; and consequently *Transubstantiation* is not proved by a Miracle, because that
would be, *to prove to a Man by something he sees, that he doth not see
what he sees.* (Ibid.)

In other words, only the observation of a miracle could establish the
doctrine of transubstantiation, but because—going back to Tillotson's
main argument—the doctrine of transubstantiation undercuts all reliance on the senses, observation could never establish the occurrence

of the miracle needed to certify this doctrine. This is ingenious, but despite its reference to a *balance* between opposing arguments, it does not exhibit the structure of Hume's reasoning concerning the balance between opposing testimony with respect to miracles. Beyond this, it is not the argument that Hume attributes to Tillotson in the opening paragraphs of "Of Miracles."

Given these disparities, both in argumentative structure and in overall intention, what are we to think of Hume's attribution of what he calls his own style of reasoning to Tillotson? I confess that I do not know the answer to this question. Perhaps Hume misremembered Tillotson's argument and simply got it wrong. If so, he was a poor scholar. It is possible that he was intentionally trying to mislead his readers into believing that the Archbishop of Canterbury sanctioned the style of arguing he was about to employ. That would make Hume a scoundrel. Perhaps Hume was doing nothing more than having mischievous fun at the archbishop's expense. Most charitably: Perhaps Hume intended no more than a general comparison between his treatment of miracles and Tillotson's treatment of transubstantiation. Hume's actual argument is similar to Tillotson's actual argument in the following way: Both approaches exploit a relationship between a concept and the testimony needed to show that something actually satisfies the concept. Hume and Tillotson do not, however, exploit this relationship in the same way. Hume's central argument, as I have represented it, is that, given the nature of a miracle, the standards for testimony establishing one must be extremely high. Tillotson argues that accepting the doctrine of transubstantiation leads to a skepticism that undercuts all testimony. In any case, both arguments turn crucially on a relationship between testimony and concepts. There seems to be no similarity deeper than this. If so, Hume's invocation of Tillotson is either overblown or ironic.[32]

Appendix 2

*"Of Miracles"*_*

PART I.

[1] THERE is, in Dr. TILLOTSON's writings, an argument against the *real presence*, which is as concise, and elegant, and strong as any argument can possibly be supposed against a doctrine, so little worthy of a serious refutation. It is acknowledged on all hands, says that learned prelate, that the authority, either of the scripture or of tradition, is founded merely in the testimony of the apostles, who were eye-witnesses to those miracles of our SAVIOUR, by which he proved his divine mission. Our evidence, then, for the truth of the CHRISTIAN religion is less than the evidence for the truth of our senses; because, even in the first authors of our religion, it was no greater; and it is evident it must diminish in passing from them to their disciples; nor can any one rest such confidence in their testimony, as in the immediate object of his senses. But a weaker evidence can never destroy a stronger; and therefore, were the doctrine of the real presence ever so clearly revealed in scripture, it were directly contrary to the rules of just reasoning to give our assent to it. It contradicts sense, though both the scripture and tradition, on which it is supposed to be built, carry not such evidence with them as sense; when they are considered merely as external evidences, and are not brought home to every one's breast, by the immediate operation of the Holy Spirit.

*Except for the removal of symbols related to an accompanying commentary and the deletion of editorial comments in footnotes, this text conforms closely to the 1999 edition of *An Enquiry concerning Human Understanding* edited by Tom L. Beauchamp, published by the Oxford University Press. Reprinted by permission of Oxford University Press.

[2] Nothing is so convenient as a decisive argument of this kind, which must at least *silence* the most arrogant bigotry and superstition, and free us from their impertinent solicitations. I flatter myself, that I have discovered an argument of a like nature, which, if just, will, with the wise and learned, be an everlasting check to all kinds of superstitious delusion, and consequently, will be useful as long as the world endures. For so long, I presume, will the accounts of miracles and prodigies be found in all history, sacred and profane.

[3] Though experience be our only guide in reasoning concerning matters of fact; it must be acknowledged, that this guide is not altogether infallible, but in some cases is apt to lead us into errors. One, who, in our climate, should expect better weather in any week of JUNE than in one of DECEMBER, would reason justly, and conformably to experience; but it is certain, that he may happen, in the event, to find himself mistaken. However, we may observe, that, in such a case, he would have no cause to complain of experience; because it commonly informs us beforehand of the uncertainty, by that contrariety of events, which we may learn from a diligent observation. All effects follow not with like certainty from their supposed causes. Some events are found, in all countries and all ages, to have been constantly conjoined together: Others are found to have been more variable, and sometimes to disappoint our expectations; so that, in our reasonings concerning matter of fact, there are all imaginable degrees of assurance, from the highest certainty to the lowest species of moral evidence.

[4] A wise man, therefore, proportions his belief to the evidence. In such conclusions as are founded on an infallible experience, he expects the event with the last degree of assurance, and regards his past experience as a full *proof* of the future existence of that event. In other cases, he proceeds with more caution: He weighs the opposite experiments: He considers which side is supported by the greater number of experiments: To that side he inclines, with doubt and hesitation; and when at last he fixes his judgment, the evidence exceeds not what we properly call *probability*. All probability, then, supposes an opposition of experiments and observations; where the one side is found to overbalance the other, and to produce a degree of evidence, proportioned to the superiority. A hundred instances or experiments on one side, and fifty on another, afford a doubtful expectation of any event; though a hundred uniform experiments, with only one that is contradictory, reasonably beget a pretty strong degree of assurance. In all cases, we must

balance the opposite experiments, where they are opposite, and deduct the smaller number from the greater, in order to know the exact force of the superior evidence.

[5] To apply these principles to a particular instance; we may observe, that there is no species of reasoning more common, more useful, and even necessary to human life, than that which is derived from the testimony of men, and the reports of eye-witnesses and spectators. This species of reasoning, perhaps, one may deny to be founded on the relation of cause and effect. I shall not dispute about a word. It will be sufficient to observe, that our assurance in any argument of this kind is derived from no other principle than our observation of the veracity of human testimony, and of the usual conformity of facts to the reports of witnesses. It being a general maxim, that no objects have any discoverable connexion together, and that all the inferences, which we can draw from one to another, are founded merely on our experience of their constant and regular conjunction; it is evident, that we ought not to make an exception to this maxim in favour of human testimony, whose connexion with any event seems, in itself, as little necessary as any other. Were not the memory tenacious to a certain degree; had not men commonly an inclination to truth and a principle of probity; were they not sensible to shame, when detected in a falsehood: Were not these, I say, discovered by *experience* to be qualities, inherent in human nature, we should never repose the least confidence in human testimony. A man delirious, or noted for falsehood and villany, has no manner of authority with us.

[6] And as the evidence, derived from witnesses and human testimony, is founded on past experience, so it varies with the experience, and is regarded either as a *proof* or a *probability*, according as the conjunction between any particular kind of report and any kind of object has been found to be constant or variable. There are a number of circumstances to be taken into consideration in all judgments of this kind; and the ultimate standard, by which we determine all disputes, that may arise concerning them, is always derived from experience and observation. Where this experience is not entirely uniform on any side, it is attended with an unavoidable contrariety in our judgments, and with the same opposition and mutual destruction of argument as in every other kind of evidence. We frequently hesitate concerning the reports of

others. We balance the opposite circumstances, which cause any doubt or uncertainty; and when we discover a superiority on any side, we incline to it; but still with a diminution of assurance, in proportion to the force of its antagonist.

[7] This contrariety of evidence, in the present case, may be derived from several different causes; from the opposition of contrary testimony; from the character or number of the witnesses; from the manner of their delivering their testimony; or from the union of all these circumstances. We entertain a suspicion concerning any matter of fact, when the witnesses contradict each other; when they are but few, or of a doubtful character; when they have an interest in what they affirm; when they deliver their testimony with hesitation, or on the contrary, with too violent asseverations. There are many other particulars of the same kind, which may diminish or destroy the force of any argument, derived from human testimony.

[8] Suppose, for instance, that the fact, which the testimony endeavours to establish, partakes of the extraordinary and the marvellous; in that case, the evidence, resulting from the testimony, admits of a diminution, greater or less, in proportion as the fact is more or less unusual. The reason, why we place any credit in witnesses and historians, is not derived from any *connexion*, which we perceive *a priori*, between testimony and reality, but because we are accustomed to find a conformity between them. But when the fact attested is such a one as has seldom fallen under our observation, here is a contest of two opposite experiences; of which the one destroys the other, as far as its force goes, and the superior can only operate on the mind by the force, which remains. The very same principle of experience, which gives us a certain degree of assurance in the testimony of witnesses, gives us also, in this case, another degree of assurance against the fact, which they endeavour to establish; from which contradiction there necessarily arises a counterpoise, and mutual destruction of belief and authority.

[9] *I should not believe such a story were it told me by* CATO; was a proverbial saying in ROME, even during the lifetime of that philosophical patriot. The incredibility of a fact, it was allowed, might invalidate so great an authority.[1]

[10] The INDIAN prince, who refused to believe the first relations concerning the effects of frost, reasoned justly; and it naturally required

very strong testimony to engage his assent to facts, that arose from a state of nature, with which he was unacquainted, and which bore so little analogy to those events, of which he had had constant and uniform experience. Though they were not contrary to his experience, they were not conformable to it.[2]

[11] But in order to encrease the probability against the testimony of witnesses, let us suppose, that the fact, which they affirm, instead of being only marvellous, is really miraculous; and suppose also, that the testimony, considered apart and in itself, amounts to an entire proof; in that case, there is proof against proof, of which the strongest must prevail, but still with a diminution of its force, in proportion to that of its antagonist.

[12] A miracle is a violation of the laws of nature; and as a firm and unalterable experience has established these laws, the proof against a miracle, from the very nature of the fact, is as entire as any argument from experience can possibly be imagined. Why is it more than probable, that all men must die; that lead cannot, of itself, remain suspended in the air; that fire consumes wood, and is extinguished by water; unless it be, that these events are found agreeable to the laws of nature, and there is required a violation of these laws, or in other words, a miracle to prevent them? Nothing is esteemed a miracle, if it ever happen in the common course of nature. It is no miracle that a man, seemingly in good health, should die on a sudden; because such a kind of death, though more unusual than any other, has yet been frequently observed to happen. But it is a miracle, that a dead man should come to life; because that has never been observed, in any age or country. There must, therefore, be a uniform experience against every miraculous event, otherwise the event would not merit that appellation. And as a uniform experience amounts to a proof, there is here a direct and full *proof*, from the nature of the fact, against the existence of any miracle; nor can such a proof be destroyed, or the miracle rendered credible, but by an opposite proof, which is superior.[3]

[13] The plain consequence is (and it is a general maxim worthy of our attention), "That no testimony is sufficient to establish a miracle, unless the testimony be of such a kind, that its falsehood would be more miraculous, than the fact, which it endeavours to establish: And even in that case, there is a mutual destruction of arguments, and the superior only gives us an assurance suitable to that degree of force, which remains, after deducting the inferior." When any one tells me, that he

saw a dead man restored to life, I immediately consider with myself, whether it be more probable, that this person should either deceive or be deceived, or that the fact, which he relates, should really have happened. I weigh the one miracle against the other; and according to the superiority, which I discover, I pronounce my decision, and always reject the greater miracle. If the falsehood of his testimony would be more miraculous, than the event which he relates; then, and not till then, can he pretend to command my belief or opinion.

PART II.

[14] In the foregoing reasoning we have supposed, that the testimony, upon which a miracle is founded, may possibly amount to an entire proof, and that the falsehood of that testimony would be a real prodigy: But it is easy to show, that we have been a great deal too liberal in our concession, and that there never was a miraculous event established on so full an evidence.

[15] For *first*, there is not to be found, in all history, any miracle attested by a sufficient number of men, of such unquestioned good sense, education, and learning, as to secure us against all delusion in themselves; of such undoubted integrity, as to place them beyond all suspicion of any design to deceive others; of such credit and reputation in the eyes of mankind, as to have a great deal to lose in case of their being detected in any falsehood; and at the same time, attesting facts, performed in such a public manner, and in so celebrated a part of the world, as to render the detection unavoidable: All which circumstances are requisite to give us a full assurance in the testimony of men.

[16] *Secondly.* We may observe in human nature a principle, which, if strictly examined, will be found to diminish extremely the assurance, which we might, from human testimony, have, in any kind of prodigy. The maxim, by which we commonly conduct ourselves in our reasonings, is, that the objects, of which we have no experience, resemble those, of which we have; that what we have found to be most usual is always most probable; and that where there is an opposition of arguments, we ought to give the preference to such as are founded on the greatest number of past observations. But though, in proceeding by this rule, we readily reject any fact which is unusual and incredible in an ordinary degree; yet in advancing farther, the mind observes not

always the same rule; but when anything is affirmed utterly absurd and miraculous, it rather the more readily admits of such a fact, upon account of that very circumstance, which ought to destroy all its authority. The passion of *surprize* and *wonder*, arising from miracles, being an agreeable emotion, gives a sensible tendency towards the belief of those events, from which it is derived. And this goes so far, that even those who cannot enjoy this pleasure immediately, nor can believe those miraculous events, of which they are informed, yet love to partake of the satisfaction at second-hand or by rebound, and place a pride and delight in exciting the admiration of others.

[17] With what greediness are the miraculous accounts of travellers received, their descriptions of sea and land monsters, their relations of wonderful adventures, strange men, and uncouth manners? But if the spirit of religion join itself to the love of wonder, there is an end of common sense; and human testimony, in these circumstances, loses all pretensions to authority. A religionist may be an enthusiast, and imagine he sees what has no reality: He may know his narrative to be false, and yet persevere in it, with the best intentions in the world, for the sake of promoting so holy a cause: Or even where this delusion has no place, vanity, excited by so strong a temptation, operates on him more powerfully than on the rest of mankind in any other circumstances; and self-interest with equal force. His auditors may not have, and commonly have not, sufficient judgment to canvass his evidence: What judgment they have, they renounce by principle, in these sublime and mysterious subjects: Or if they were ever so willing to employ it, passion and a heated imagination disturb the regularity of its operations. Their credulity encreases his impudence: And his impudence overpowers their credulity.

[18] Eloquence, when at its highest pitch, leaves little room for reason or reflection; but addressing itself entirely to the fancy or the affections, captivates the willing hearers, and subdues their understanding. Happily, this pitch it seldom attains. But what a TULLY or a DEMOSTHENES could scarcely effect over a ROMAN or ATHENIAN audience, every *Capuchin*, every itinerant or stationary teacher can perform over the generality of mankind, and in a higher degree, by touching such gross and vulgar passions.

[19] The many instances of forged miracles, and prophecies, and supernatural events, which, in all ages, have either been detected by contrary evidence, or which detect themselves by their absurdity, prove

sufficiently the strong propensity of mankind to the extraordinary and the marvellous, and ought reasonably to beget a suspicion against all relations of this kind. This is our natural way of thinking, even with regard to the most common and most credible events. For instance: There is no kind of report, which rises so easily, and spreads so quickly, especially in country places and provincial towns, as those concerning marriages; insomuch that two young persons of equal condition never see each other twice, but the whole neighbourhood immediately join them together. The pleasure of telling a piece of news so interesting, of propagating it, and of being the first reporters of it, spreads the intelligence. And this is so well known, that no man of sense gives attention to these reports, till he find them confirmed by some greater evidence. Do not the same passions, and others still stronger, incline the generality of mankind to believe and report, with the greatest vehemence and assurance, all religious miracles?

[20] *Thirdly*, It forms a strong presumption against all supernatural and miraculous relations, that they are observed chiefly to abound among ignorant and barbarous nations; or if a civilized people has ever given admission to any of them, that people will be found to have received them from ignorant and barbarous ancestors, who transmitted them with that inviolable sanction and authority, which always attend received opinions. When we peruse the first histories of all nations, we are apt to imagine ourselves transported into some new world; where the whole frame of nature is disjointed, and every element performs its operations in a different manner, from what it does at present. Battles, revolutions, pestilence, famine, and death, are never the effect of those natural causes, which we experience. Prodigies, omens, oracles, judgments, quite obscure the few natural events, that are intermingled with them. But as the former grow thinner every page, in proportion as we advance nearer the enlightened ages, we soon learn, that there is nothing mysterious or supernatural in the case, but that all proceeds from the usual propensity of mankind towards the marvellous, and that, though this inclination may at intervals receive a check from sense and learning, it can never be thoroughly extirpated from human nature.

[21] *It is strange*, a judicious reader is apt to say, upon the perusal of these wonderful historians, *that such prodigious events never happen in our days*. But it is nothing strange, I hope, that men should lie in all ages. You must surely have seen instances enough of that frailty. You have yourself heard many such marvellous relations started, which,

being treated with scorn by all the wise and judicious, have at last been abandoned even by the vulgar. Be assured, that those renowned lies, which have spread and flourished to such a monstrous height, arose from like beginnings; but being sown in a more proper soil, shot up at last into prodigies almost equal to those which they relate.

[22] It was a wise policy in that false prophet, ALEXANDER, who, though now forgotten, was once so famous, to lay the first scene of his impostures in PAPHLAGONIA, where, as LUCIAN tells us, the people were extremely ignorant and stupid, and ready to swallow even the grossest delusion. People at a distance, who are weak enough to think the matter at all worth enquiry, have no opportunity of receiving better information. The stories come magnified to them by a hundred circumstances. Fools are industrious in propagating the imposture; while the wise and learned are contented, in general, to deride its absurdity, without informing themselves of the particular facts, by which it may be distinctly refuted. And thus the impostor above-mentioned was enabled to proceed, from his ignorant PAPHLAGONIANS, to the enlisting of votaries, even among the GRECIAN philosophers, and men of the most eminent rank and distinction in ROME: Nay, could engage the attention of that sage emperor MARCUS AURELIUS; so far as to make him trust the success of a military expedition to his delusive prophecies.

[23] The advantages are so great, of starting an imposture among an ignorant people, that, even though the delusion should be too gross to impose on the generality of them (*which, though seldom, is sometimes the case*) it has a much better chance for succeeding in remote countries, than if the first scene had been laid in a city renowned for arts and knowledge. The most ignorant and barbarous of these barbarians carry the report abroad. None of their countrymen have a large correspondence, or sufficient credit and authority to contradict and beat down the delusion. Men's inclination to the marvellous has full opportunity to display itself. And thus a story, which is universally exploded in the place where it was first started, shall pass for certain at a thousand miles distance. But had ALEXANDER fixed his residence at ATHENS, the philosophers of that renowned mart of learning had immediately spread, throughout the whole ROMAN empire, their sense of the matter; which, being supported by so great authority, and displayed by all the force of reason and eloquence, had entirely opened the eyes of mankind. It is true; Lucian, passing by chance through PAPHLAGONIA, had an opportunity of performing this good office. But, though much

to be wished, it does not always happen, that every ALEXANDER meets with a LUCIAN, ready to expose and detect his impostures.

[24] I may add as a *fourth* reason, which diminishes the authority of prodigies, that there is no testimony for any, even those which have not been expressly detected, that is not opposed by an infinite number of witnesses; so that not only the miracle destroys the credit of testimony, but the testimony destroys itself. To make this the better understood, let us consider, that, in matters of religion, whatever is different is contrary; and that it is impossible the religions of ancient ROME, of TURKEY, of SIAM, and of CHINA should, all of them, be established on any solid foundation. Every miracle, therefore, pretended to have been wrought in any of these religions (and all of them abound in miracles), as its direct scope is to establish the particular system to which it is attributed; so has it the same force, though more indirectly, to overthrow every other system. In destroying a rival system, it likewise destroys the credit of those miracles, on which that system was established; so that all the prodigies of different religions are to be regarded as contrary facts, and the evidences of these prodigies, whether weak or strong, as opposite to each other. According to this method of reasoning, when we believe any miracle of MAHOMET or his successors, we have for our warrant the testimony of a few barbarous ARABIANS: And on the other hand, we are to regard the authority of TITUS LIVIUS, PLUTARCH, TACITUS, and, in short, of all the authors and witnesses, GRECIAN, CHINESE, and ROMAN CATHOLIC, who have related any miracle in their particular religion; I say, we are to regard their testimony in the same light as if they had mentioned that MAHOMETAN miracle, and had in express terms contradicted it, with the same certainty as they have for the miracle they relate. This argument may appear over subtile and refined; but is not in reality different from the reasoning of a judge, who supposes, that the credit of two witnesses, maintaining a crime against any one, is destroyed by the testimony of two others, who affirm him to have been two hundred leagues distant, at the same instant when the crime is said to have been committed.

[25] One of the best attested miracles in all profane history, is that which TACITUS reports of VESPASIAN, who cured a blind man in ALEXANDRIA, by means of his spittle, and a lame man by the mere touch of his foot; in obedience to a vision of the god SERAPIS, who had enjoined them to have recourse to the Emperor, for these miraculous cures. The story may be seen in that fine historian;[4] where every circum-

stance seems to add weight to the testimony, and might be displayed
at large with all the force of argument and eloquence, if any one were
now concerned to enforce the evidence of that exploded and idolatrous
superstition. The gravity, solidity, age, and probity of so great an emperor, who, through the whole course of his life, conversed in a familiar
manner with his friends and courtiers, and never affected those extraordinary airs of divinity assumed by ALEXANDER and DEMETRIUS.
The historian, a cotemporary writer, noted for candour and veracity,
and withal, the greatest and most penetrating genius, perhaps, of all
antiquity; and so free from any tendency to credulity, that he even
lies under the contrary imputation, of atheism and profaneness: The
persons, from whose authority he related the miracle, of established
character for judgment and veracity, as we may well presume; eye-
witnesses of the fact, and confirming their testimony, after the FLAVIAN
family was despoiled of the empire, and could no longer give any re-
ward, as the price of a lie. Utrumque, qui interfuere, nunc quoque
memorant, postquam nullum mendacio pretium. [Those who were
present recount both incidents even now, when there is nothing to
gain from the deceit.] To which if we add the public nature of the
facts, as related, it will appear, that no evidence can well be supposed
stronger for so gross and so palpable a falsehood.

[26] There is also a memorable story related by Cardinal DE RETZ,
which may well deserve our consideration. When that intriguing poli-
tician fled into SPAIN, to avoid the persecution of his enemies, he passed
through SARAGOSSA, the capital of ARRAGON, where he was shown, in
the cathedral, a man, who had served seven years as a door-keeper, and
was well known to every body in town, that had ever paid his devotions
at that church. He had been seen, for so long a time, wanting a leg;
but recovered that limb by the rubbing of holy oil upon the stump;
and the cardinal assures us that he saw him with two legs. This miracle
was vouched by all the canons of the church; and the whole company
in town were appealed to for a confirmation of the fact; whom the
cardinal found, by their zealous devotion, to be thorough believers of
the miracle. Here the relater was also cotemporary to the supposed
prodigy, of an incredulous and libertine character, as well as of great
genius; the miracle of so *singular* a nature as could scarcely admit of a
counterfeit, and the witnesses very numerous, and all of them, in a
manner, spectators of the fact, to which they gave their testimony. And
what adds mightily to the force of the evidence, and may double our

surprize on this occasion, is, that the cardinal himself, who relates the
story, seems not to give any credit to it, and consequently cannot be
suspected of any concurrence in the holy fraud. He considered justly,
that it was not requisite, in order to reject a fact of this nature, to be
able accurately to disprove the testimony, and to trace its falsehood,
through all the circumstances of knavery and credulity which produced
it. He knew, that, as this was commonly altogether impossible at any
small distance of time and place; so was it extremely difficult, even
where one was immediately present, by reason of the bigotry, ignorance, cunning, and roguery of a great part of mankind. He therefore
concluded, like a just reasoner, that such an evidence carried falsehood
upon the very face of it, and that a miracle, supported by any human
testimony, was more properly a subject of derision than of argument.
[27] There surely never was a greater number of miracles ascribed to
one person, than those, which were lately said to have been wrought
in FRANCE upon the tomb of Abbé PARIS, the famous JANSENIST, with
whose sanctity the people were so long deluded. The curing of the
sick, giving hearing to the deaf, and sight to the blind, were every
where talked of as the usual effects of that holy sepulchre. But what is
more extraordinary; many of the miracles were immediately proved
upon the spot, before judges of unquestioned integrity, attested by witnesses of credit and distinction, in a learned age, and on the most eminent theatre that is now in the world. Nor is this all: A relation of them
was published and dispersed every where; nor were the JESUITS, though
a learned body, supported by the civil magistrate, and determined enemies to those opinions, in whose favour the miracles were said to have
been wrought, ever able distinctly to refute or detect them.[5] Where
shall we find such a number of circumstances, agreeing to the corroboration of one fact? And what have we to oppose to such a cloud of
witnesses, but the absolute impossibility or miraculous nature of the
events, which they relate? And this surely, in the eyes of all reasonable
people, will alone be regarded as a sufficient refutation.
[28] Is the consequence just, because some human testimony has the
utmost force and authority in some cases, when it relates the battle of
PHILIPPI or PHARSALIA for instance; that therefore all kinds of testimony must, in all cases, have equal force and authority? Suppose that
the CAESAREAN and POMPEIAN factions had, each of them, claimed the
victory in these battles, and that the historians of each party had uniformly ascribed the advantage to their own side; how could mankind,

at this distance, have been able to determine between them? The contrariety is equally strong between the miracles related by HERODOTUS or PLUTARCH, and those delivered by MARIANA, BEDE, or any monkish historian.

[29] The wise lend a very academic faith to every report which favours the passion of the reporter; whether it magnifies his country, his family, or himself, or in any other way strikes in with his natural inclinations and propensities. But what greater temptation than to appear a missionary, a prophet, an ambassador from heaven? Who would not encounter many dangers and difficulties, in order to attain so sublime a character? Or if, by the help of vanity and a heated imagination, a man has first made a convert of himself, and entered seriously into the delusion; who ever scruples to make use of pious frauds, in support of so holy and meritorious a cause?

[30] The smallest spark may here kindle into the greatest flame; because the materials are always prepared for it. The *avidum genus auricularum* [the tribe eager for gossip],[6] the gazing populace, receive greedily, without examination, whatever sooths superstition, and promotes wonder.

[31] How many stories of this nature have, in all ages, been detected and exploded in their infancy? How many more have been celebrated for a time, and have afterwards sunk into neglect and oblivion? Where such reports, therefore, fly about, the solution of the phenomenon is obvious; and we judge in conformity to regular experience and observation, when we account for it by the known and natural principles of credulity and delusion. And shall we, rather than have a recourse to so natural a solution, allow of a miraculous violation of the most established laws of nature?

[32] I need not mention the difficulty of detecting a falsehood in any private or even public history, at the place, where it is said to happen; much more when the scene is removed to ever so small a distance. Even a court of judicature, with all the authority, accuracy, and judgment, which they can employ, find themselves often at a loss to distinguish between truth and falsehood in the most recent actions. But the matter never comes to any issue, if trusted to the common method of altercation and debate and flying rumours; especially when men's passions have taken part on either side.

[33] In the infancy of new religions, the wise and learned commonly esteem the matter too inconsiderable to deserve their attention or re-

gard. And when afterwards they would willingly detect the cheat, in order to undeceive the deluded multitude, the season is now past, and the records and witnesses, which might clear up the matter, have perished beyond recovery.

[34] No means of detection remain, but those which must be drawn from the very testimony itself of the reporters: And these, though always sufficient with the judicious and knowing, are commonly too fine to fall under the comprehension of the vulgar.

[35] Upon the whole, then, it appears, that no testimony for any kind of miracle has ever amounted to a probability, much less to a proof; and that, even supposing it amounted to a proof, it would be opposed by another proof; derived from the very nature of the fact, which it would endeavour to establish. It is experience only, which gives authority to human testimony; and it is the same experience, which assures us of the laws of nature. When, therefore, these two kinds of experience are contrary, we have nothing to do but subtract the one from the other, and embrace an opinion, either on one side or the other, with that assurance which arises from the remainder. But according to the principle here explained, this subtraction, with regard to all popular religions, amounts to an entire annihilation; and therefore we may establish it as a maxim, that no human testimony can have such force as to prove a miracle, and make it a just foundation for any such system of religion.

[36] I beg the limitations here made may be remarked, when I say, that a miracle can never be proved, so as to be the foundation of a system of religion. For I own, that otherwise, there may possibly be miracles, or violations of the usual course of nature, of such a kind as to admit of proof from human testimony; though, perhaps, it will be impossible to find any such in all the records of history. Thus, suppose, all authors, in all languages, agree, that, from the first of JANUARY 1600, there was a total darkness over the whole earth for eight days: Suppose that the tradition of this extraordinary event is still strong and lively among the people: That all travellers, who return from foreign countries, bring us accounts of the same tradition, without the least variation or contradiction: It is evident, that our present philosophers, instead of doubting the fact, ought to receive it as certain, and ought to search for the causes whence it might be derived. The decay, corruption, and dissolution of nature, is an event rendered probable by so many analogies, that any phenomenon, which seems to have a tendency towards

that catastrophe, comes within the reach of human testimony, if that testimony be very extensive and uniform.

[37] But suppose, that all the historians, who treat of ENGLAND, should agree, that, on the first of JANUARY 1600, Queen ELIZABETH died; that both before and after her death she was seen by her physicians and the whole court, as is usual with persons of her rank; that her successor was acknowledged and proclaimed by the parliament; and that, after being interred a month, she again appeared, resumed the throne, and governed ENGLAND for three years: I must confess that I should be surprized at the concurrence of so many odd circumstances, but should not have the least inclination to believe so miraculous an event. I should not doubt of her pretended death, and of those other public circumstances that followed it: I should only assert it to have been pretended, and that it neither was, nor possibly could be real. You would in vain object to me the difficulty, and almost impossibility of deceiving the world in an affair of such consequence; the wisdom and solid judgment of that renowned queen; with the little or no advantage which she could reap from so poor an artifice: All this might astonish me; but I would still reply, that the knavery and folly of men are such common phenomena, that I should rather believe the most extraordinary events to arise from their concurrence, than admit of so signal a violation of the laws of nature.

[38] But should this miracle be ascribed to any new system of religion; men, in all ages, have been so much imposed on by ridiculous stories of that kind, that this very circumstance would be a full proof of a cheat, and sufficient, with all men of sense, not only to make them reject the fact, but even reject it without farther examination. Though the Being, to whom the miracle is ascribed, be, in this case, Almighty, it does not, upon that account, become a whit more probable; since it is impossible for us to know the attributes or actions of such a Being, otherwise than from the experience which we have of his productions, in the usual course of nature. This still reduces us to past observation, and obliges us to compare the instances of the violations of truth in the testimony of men with those of the violations of the laws of nature by miracles, in order to judge which of them is most likely and probable. As the violations of truth are more common in the testimony concerning religious miracles, than in that concerning any other matter

of fact; this must diminish very much the authority of the former testimony, and make us form a general resolution, never to lend any attention to it, with whatever specious pretence it may be covered.

[39] Lord BACON seems to have embraced the same principles of reasoning. "We ought," says he, "to make a collection or particular history of all monsters and prodigious births or productions, and in a word of every thing new, rare, and extraordinary in nature. But this must be done with the most severe scrutiny, lest we depart from truth. Above all, every relation must be considered as suspicious, which depends in any degree upon religion, as the prodigies of LIVY: And no less so, every thing that is to be found in the writers of natural magic or alchimy, or such authors, who seem, all of them, to have an unconquerable appetite for falsehood and fable."[7]

[40] I am the better pleased with the method of reasoning here delivered, as I think it may serve to confound those dangerous friends or disguised enemies to the CHRISTIAN religion, who have undertaken to defend it by the principles of human reason. Our most holy religion is founded on *Faith*, not on reason; and it is a sure method of exposing it to put it to such a trial as it is, by no means, fitted to endure. To make this more evident, let us examine those miracles, related in scripture; and not to lose ourselves in too wide a field, let us confine ourselves to such as we find in the *Pentateuch*, which we shall examine, according to the principles of these pretended CHRISTIANS, not as the word or testimony of God himself, but as the production of a mere human writer and historian. Here then we are first to consider a book, presented to us by a barbarous and ignorant people, written in an age when they were still more barbarous, and in all probability long after the facts which it relates, corroborated by no concurring testimony, and resembling those fabulous accounts, which every nation gives of its origin. Upon reading this book, we find it full of prodigies and miracles. It gives an account of a state of the world and of human nature entirely different from the present: Of our fall from that state: Of the age of man, extended to near a thousand years: Of the destruction of the world by a deluge: Of the arbitrary choice of one people, as the favourites of heaven; and that people the countrymen of the author: Of their deliverance from bondage by prodigies the most astonishing imaginable: I desire any one to lay his hand upon his heart,

and after a serious consideration declare, whether he thinks that the falsehood of such a book, supported by such a testimony, would be more extraordinary and miraculous than all the miracles it relates; which is, however, necessary to make it be received, according to the measures of probability above established.

[41] What we have said of miracles may be applied, without any variation, to prophecies; and indeed, all prophecies are real miracles, and as such only, can be admitted as proofs of any revelation. If it did not exceed the capacity of human nature to foretel future events, it would be absurd to employ any prophecy as an argument for a divine mission or authority from heaven. So that, upon the whole, we may conclude, that the CHRISTIAN religion not only was at first attended with miracles, but even at this day cannot be believed by any reasonable person without one. Mere reason is insufficient to convince us of its veracity: And whoever is moved by *Faith* to assent to it, is conscious of a continued miracle in his own person, which subverts all the principles of his understanding, and gives him a determination to believe what is most contrary to custom and experience.

HUME'S FOOTNOTES

1. PLUTARCH, in vita CATONIS.

2. No INDIAN, it is evident, could have experience that water did not freeze in cold climates. This is placing nature in a situation quite unknown to him; and it is impossible for him to tell *a priori* what will result from it. It is making a new experiment, the consequence of which is always uncertain. One may sometimes conjecture from analogy what will follow; but still this is but conjecture. And it must be confessed, that, in the present case of freezing, the event follows contrary to the rules of analogy, and is such as a rational INDIAN would not look for. The operations of cold upon water are not gradual, according to the degrees of cold; but whenever it comes to the freezing point, the water passes in a moment, from the utmost liquidity to perfect hardness. Such an event, therefore, may be denominated *extraordinary*, and requires a pretty strong testimony, to render it credible to people in a warm climate: But still it is not *miraculous*, nor contrary to uniform experience of the course of nature in cases where all the circumstances are the same. The inhabitants of SUMATRA have always seen water fluid in their own climate, and the freezing of their rivers ought to be deemed a prodigy: But they never saw water in MUSCOVY

during the winter; and therefore they cannot reasonably be positive what would there be the consequence.

3. Sometimes an event may not, *in itself*, *seem* to be contrary to the laws of nature, and yet, if it were real, it might, by reason of some circumstances, be denominated a miracle; because, in *fact*, it is contrary to these laws. Thus if a person, claiming a divine authority, should command a sick person to be well, a healthful man to fall down dead, the clouds to pour rain, the winds to blow, in short, should order many natural events, which immediately follow upon his command; these might justly be esteemed miracles, because they are really, in this case, contrary to the laws of nature. For if any suspicion remain, that the event and command concurred by accident, there is no miracle and no transgression of the laws of nature. If this suspicion be removed, there is evidently a miracle, and a transgression of these laws; because nothing can be more contrary to nature than that the voice or command of a man should have such an influence. A miracle may be accurately defined, *a transgression of a law of nature by a particular volition of the Deity, or by the interposition of some invisible agent.* A miracle may either be discoverable by men or not. This alters not its nature and essence. The raising of a house or ship into the air is a visible miracle. The raising of a feather, when the wind wants ever so little of a force requisite for that purpose, is as real a miracle, though not so sensible with regard to us.

4. Hist. lib. 4. cap. 81. SUETONIUS gives nearly the same account in vita VESP.

5. This book was writ by Mons. MONTGERON, counsellor or judge of the parliament of PARIS, a man of figure and character, who was also a martyr to the cause, and is now said to be somewhere in a dungeon on account of his book.

There is another book in three volumes (called *Recueil des Miracles de l'Abbé* PARIS) giving an account of many of these miracles, and accompanied with prefatory discourses, which are very well written. There runs, however, through the whole of these a ridiculous comparison between the miracles of our Savior and those of the Abbé; wherein it is asserted, that the evidence for the latter is equal to that for the former: As if the testimony of men could ever be put in the balance with that of God himself, who conducted the pen of the inspired writers. If these writers, indeed, were to be considered merely as human testimony, the FRENCH author is very moderate in his comparison; since he might, with some appearance of reason, pretend, that the JANSENIST miracles much surpass the other in evidence and authority. The following circumstances are drawn from authentic papers, inserted in the above-mentioned book.

Many of the miracles of Abbé PARIS were proved immediately by witnesses before the officiality or bishop's court at PARIS, under the eye of Cardinal NOAILLES, whose character for integrity and capacity was never contested even by his enemies.

His successor in the archbishopric was an enemy to the Jansenists, and for that reason promoted to the see by the court. Yet 22 rectors or *curés* of Paris, with infinite earnestness, press him to examine those miracles, which they assert to be known to the whole world, and undisputably certain: But he wisely forbore.

The Molinist party had tried to discredit these miracles in one instance, that of Madamoiselle Le Franc. But, besides that their proceedings were in many respects the most irregular in the world, particularly in citing only a few of the Jansenist witnesses, whom they tampered with: Besides this, I say, they soon found themselves overwhelmed by a cloud of new witnesses, one hundred and twenty in number, most of them persons of credit and substance in Paris, who gave oath for the miracle. This was accompanied with a solemn and earnest appeal to the parliament. But the parliament were forbid by authority to meddle in the affair. It was at last observed, that where men are heated by zeal and enthusiasm, there is no degree of human testimony so strong as may not be procured for the greatest absurdity: And those who will be so silly as to examine the affair by that medium, and seek particular flaws in the testimony, are almost sure to be confounded. It must be a miserable imposture, indeed, that does not prevail in that contest.

All who have been in France about that time have heard of the reputation of Mons. Heraut, the *Lieutenant de Police*, whose vigilance, penetration, activity, and extensive intelligence have been much talked of. This magistrate, who by the nature of his office is almost absolute, was invested with full powers, on purpose to suppress or discredit these miracles; and he frequently seized immediately, and examined the witnesses and subjects of them: But never could reach any thing satisfactory against them.

In the case of Madamoiselle Thibault he sent the famous De Sylva to examine her; whose evidence is very curious. The physician declares, that it was impossible she could have been so ill as was proved by witnesses; because it was impossible she could, in so short a time, have recovered so perfectly as he found her. He reasoned, like a man of sense, from natural causes; but the opposite party told him, that the whole was a miracle, and that his evidence was the very best proof of it.

The Molinists were in a sad dilemma. They durst not assert the absolute insufficiency of human evidence, to prove a miracle. They were obliged to say, that these miracles were wrought by witchcraft and the devil. But they were told, that this was the resource of the Jews of old.

No Jansenist was ever embarrassed to account for the cessation of the miracles, when the church-yard was shut up by the king's edict. It was the touch of the tomb, which produced these extraordinary effects; and when no one could approach the tomb, no effects could be expected. God, indeed, could have thrown down the walls in a moment; but he is master of his own graces and works, and it belongs not to us to account for them. He did not throw down the walls of every city like those of JERICHO, on the sounding of the rams' horns, nor break up the prison of every apostle, like that of ST. PAUL.

No less a man, than the Duc de CHATILLON, a duke and peer of FRANCE, of the highest rank and family, gives evidence of a miraculous cure, performed upon a servant of his, who had lived several years in his house with a visible and palpable infirmity.

I shall conclude with observing, that no clergy are more celebrated for strictness of life and manners than the secular clergy of FRANCE, particularly the rectors or curés of PARIS, who bear testimony to these impostures.

The learning, genius, and probity of the gentlemen, and the austerity of the nuns of PORT-ROYAL, have been much celebrated all over EUROPE. Yet they all give evidence for a miracle, wrought on the niece of the famous PASCAL, whose sanctity of life, as well as extraordinary capacity, is well known. The famous RACINE gives an account of this miracle in his famous history of PORT-ROYAL, and fortifies it with all the proofs, which a multitude of nuns, priests, physicians, and men of the world, all of them of undoubted credit, could bestow upon it. Several men of letters, particularly the bishop of TOURNAY, thought this miracle so certain, as to employ it in the refutation of atheists and free-thinkers. The queen-regent of FRANCE, who was extremely prejudiced against the PORT-ROYAL, sent her own physician to examine the miracle, who returned an absolute convert. In short, the supernatural cure was so uncontestable, that it saved, for a time, that famous monastery from the ruin with which it was threatened by the JESUITS. Had it been a cheat, it had certainly been detected by such sagacious and powerful antagonists, and must have hastened the ruin of the contrivers. Our divines, who can build up a formidable castle from such despicable materials; what a prodigious fabric could they have reared from these and many other circumstances, which I have not mentioned! How often would the great names of PASCAL, RACINE, ARNAULD, NICOLE, have resounded in our ears? But if they be wise, they had better adopt the miracle, as being more worth, a thousand times, than all the rest of their collection. Besides, it may serve very much to their purpose. For that miracle was really performed by the touch of an authentic holy prickle of the holy thorn, which composed the holy crown, which, &c.

6. LUCRET.

7. Nov. Org. lib. 2. aph. 29.

Notes

1. In a letter to Henry Home, Hume explains his reasons for not including a section on miracles in his *Treatise of Human Nature* as follows:

> [I] enclose some Reasonings concerning Miracles, which I once thought of publishing with the rest, but which I am afraid will give too much offence, even as the world is disposed at present. . . . Your thoughts and mine agree with respect to Dr Butler and I would be glad to be introduced to him. I am at present castrating my work, that is, cutting off its nobler parts; that is, endeavouring it shall give as little offence as possible, before which, I could not pretend to put it into the Doctor's hands. This is a piece of cowardice, for which I blame myself, though I believe none of my friends will blame me. But I was resolved not to be an enthusiast in philosophy, while I was blaming other enthusiasms. (Hume 1932, letter 6)

2. Hume cites John Tillotson's attack on the Roman Catholic doctrine of the real presence (transubstantiation) as the inspiration for his own reasoning concerning the evaluation of testimony brought forth in behalf of miracles. There is something of a mystery here, for, as a number of writers have noted, the argument that Hume attributes to Tillotson cannot be found in that author's work. Beyond this, Hume's treatment of miracles actually runs counter to Tillotson's central argumentative move. I have tried to sort out Hume's relationship to Tillotson—and, along the way, exhibit Tillotson's polemical skills—in appendix 1 to this work.

3. This Humean or inductive approach to the evaluation of testimony has been challenged by a number of philosophers who have offered something like a transcendental argument to the effect that testimony as such carries with it a presumption of reliability—a presumption, however, that can be overridden. See, for example, Coady (1992). There is, however, no need to choose between these

approaches here, because Hume's reflections on miracles can be presented equally well on either.

4. Don Garrett called my attention to these passages in Locke. Middleton's *Free Inquiry* invokes these two standards as well:

> The present question, concerning the reality of the miraculous powers of the primitive Church, depends on the joint credibility of the facts, pretended to have been produced by those powers, and of the witnesses, who attest them. (Middleton 1749, ix)

Concerning the credibility of witnesses, Middleton spends a great deal of time arguing that there seemed no limit to the unsubstantiated claims that the church fathers were willing to accept. Concerning the credibility of the miraculous events themselves, Middleton relies mainly on their contrived, bizarre, even tasteless character as providing sufficient grounds for anyone of good sense to reject them. To this end he cites a long series of supposedly miraculous events and allows their inherent implausibility to speak for itself. His account of the martyrdom of Saint Polycarp is particularly noteworthy in this respect. See Middleton (1749, 124–25).

A parallel discussion of these two kinds of standards for evaluating testimony is found in chapter 13 of the fourth part of the *Logic or the Art of Thinking* (*The Port-Royal Logic*). There Antoine Arnauld, who wrote this portion of the text, tells us, "In order to decide the truth about an event and to determine whether or not to believe in it, . . . we must pay attention to all the accompanying circumstances, internal as well as external. I call those circumstances internal that belong to the fact itself, and those external that concern the persons whose testimony leads us to believe in it" (Arnauld and Nicole 1996, 264). In the chapter that follows, Arnauld uses these standards in an attempt to show that some—but, just as importantly, not all—testimony in behalf of miracles can pass muster. He looks with particular favor on miracles recorded in the writings of Saint Augustine, some of which Middleton singles out as being particularly contemptible. See Middleton (1749, 141 ff.).

5. If we have independent reason to think that a deity exists who sometimes sees fit to produce miracles for special purposes, then invoking the action of such a being might provide the best explanation for miraculous occurrences. This move would not be permitted, though, if the supposed occurrence of a miracle were being cited as proof of God's existence. Hume, as we shall see, quite specially targets reports of miracles intended to serve, as he says, as a "foundation" for a system of religion.

6. Hume adds a perplexing footnote at this point that I will cite in full:

Sometimes an event may not, *in itself, seem* to be contrary to the laws of nature, and yet, if it were real, it might, by reason of some circumstances, be denominated a miracle; because, in *fact*, it is contrary to these laws. Thus if a person, claiming a divine authority, should command a sick person to be well, a healthful man to fall down dead, the clouds to pour rain, the winds to blow, in short, should order many natural events, which immediately follow upon his command; these might justly be esteemed miracles, because they are really, in this case, contrary to the laws of nature. For if any suspicion remain, that the event and command concurred by accident, there is no miracle and no transgression of the laws of nature. If this suspicion be removed, there is evidently a miracle, and a transgression of these laws; because nothing can be more contrary to nature than that the voice or command of a man should have such an influence. A miracle may be accurately defined, *a transgression of a law of nature by a particular volition of the Deity, or by the interposition of some invisible agent*. A miracle may either be discoverable by men or not. This alters not its nature and essence. The raising of a house or ship into the air is a visible miracle. The raising of a feather, when the wind wants ever so little of a force requisite for that purpose, is as real a miracle, though not so sensible with regard to us. (*EHU*, 10 n. 23)

When Hume says that a "miracle may be accurately defined, a transgression of a law of nature by a particular volition of the Deity, or by the interposition of some invisible agent," he seems to be making the intervention of a divine (or at least invisible) agent an essential feature of a miracle. Yet elsewhere, indeed, even in this very footnote, Hume uses the notion of a miracle in a wider sense that includes the notion of nonreligious miracles. The discussion in part 2 relies on this contrast between religious and nonreligious miracles. It seems, then, that Hume's intention here cannot be to narrow the notion of a miracle to religious miracles, but only to define one particular kind of miracle— those that are supposed to depend upon divine intervention.

7. See Fogelin (1994), particularly chapters 1 and 5.

8. This misreading is found, for example, in Fogelin (1990). This error was largely due to a failure on my part to appreciate what Hume means by a proof.

9. Though the notions of being question-begging and being circular are often used interchangeably, I am inclined to think that circularity is a logical property of arguments or proofs, whereas question-begging is a property of debates. In this context I will not press this difference because it should become clear that Hume neither reasons in a circle nor begs any questions.

10. More recently, David Johnson (1999) has given this criticism a more elaborate statement by maintaining that Hume's argument and its various reconstructions invariably go wrong in one of two ways: either (i) they are circular in something like the way that Johnson suggests, or (ii) in their attempts to avoid circularity, they lose their power to establish their conclusion. I consider and reject Johnson's criticisms in chapter 2.

11. At least with respect to the church fathers, Middleton is even more dismissive.

> I have shown, by many indisputable facts, that the ancient Fathers . . . were extremely credulous and superstitious; possessed with strong prejudices and an enthusiastic zeal, in favor, not only of Christianity in general, but of every particular doctrine, which a wild imagination could ingraft upon it; and scrupling no art or means, by which they might propagate the same principles. (Middleton 1749, xxxi–xxxii)

12. He makes this same point in the *Treatise*, where he cites the tendency to accept accounts of miracles as illustrative of his own theory of belief: "The first astonishment, which naturally attends their miraculous relations, spreads itself over the whole soul, and so vivifies and enlivens the idea, that it resembles the inferences we draw from experience. This is a mystery, with which we may be already a little acquainted, and which we shall have farther occasion to be let into in the progress of this Treatise" (*THN*, 1.3.10.4). The further occasion alluded to here does not appear in the *Treatise*.

13. This reappearance of the central argument of part 1 tucked away in a subargument of part 2 invites the speculation—and it can be no more than a speculation—that part 2, except for its opening paragraph, was a complete essay written before part 1.

14. Hume does not actually say what laws of nature are broken in his example. Perhaps he had nothing more in mind than the orderly succession of night and day. It is also easy to think of naturalistic explanations of the phenomenon in question: clouds from massive volcanic eruptions, or the impact of a comet; perhaps a black hole passed by Earth, sucking up all the incoming light. It would, however, be easy enough to fill out Hume's example in ways that would make it transparently clear that certain well-established laws of nature had been violated.

15. In the following passage, Hume certainly seems to be speaking of a law as a regularity in nature—specifically of a regularity unknown to us.

[Physicians] know, that a human body is a mighty complicated machine: That many secret powers lurk in it, which are altogether beyond our comprehension: That to us it must often appear very uncertain in its operations: And that therefore the irregular events, which outwardly discover themselves, can be no proof, that the laws of nature are not observed with the greatest regularity in its internal operations and government. (*EHU*, 8.14)

16. Earman (2000, 23) himself cites this letter, but not this passage.

17. In this passage Earman is specifically discussing a reading of Hume's text found in the writings of both Richard Price and C. D. Broad. Because the point he is making is completely general, I have deleted these references.

18. J. H. Sobel, rightly I think, describes Hume as an intuitive Bayesian (Sobel 1987, 166–86). David Owen argues that Hume's treatment of miracles "can best be seen as applying a proto-Baysean argument to a celebrated eighteenth-century argument" (Owen 1987, 187). More strikingly, Owen shows that Hume's notion of balancing proof against proof has the underlying form of Bayes's theorem and, in fact, using Bayes's theorem, yields just the results that Hume espouses (ibid., 191–92).

19. See Earman (2000, 26–27).

20. I made some tentative suggestions in this direction in Fogelin (1985, 58–60). This claim has been defended in detail in Mura (1998), and more fully in Mura (1996).

21. See, for example, Tversky and Kahneman (1982).

22. Hume uses this wording in *An Abstract of a Treatise of Human Nature*, which can be found an appendix to *A Treatise of Human Nature* (*THN, Abstract*, 14), and in the *Enquiry concerning Human Understanding* (*EHU*, 4.18). The claim is made in a slightly different way in *A Treatise of Human Nature* (*THN*, 1.3.6.5).

23. See chapter 2 of Fogelin (1985).

24. Cited by Earman (2000, 31).

25. Earman defines a Hume miracle to be "an event that has a faithful description *M* such that *M* contradicts some presumptive law statement" (ibid., 12). This is, in essence, the way I understand a miracle as well.

26. I do not see why the loss of a sharp distinction between marvels and miracles makes any difference to Hume's argument, unless he is employing some version of the definitional argument, which, as I have argued, he is not.

27. I discuss the relationship between Hume's skepticism and his naturalistic account of the human mind in Fogelin (1985).

28. Hume does not hold that causal explanations of human actions are always simple and easy to discover. In the physical sciences and the social sciences alike, causal explanations become more complex and less easily found as the number of relevant causal factors increases.

> We must not, however, expect, that this uniformity of human actions should be carried to such a length, as that all men, in the same circumstances, will always act precisely in the same manner, without making any allowance for the diversity of characters, prejudices, and opinions. *Such a uniformity in every particular, is found in no part of nature.* On the contrary, from observing the variety of conduct in different men, we are enabled to form a greater variety of maxims, which still suppose a degree of uniformity and regularity. (*EHU*, 8.10, emphasis added)

29. There is no reason why Hume could not examine the influence of *beliefs* in miracles from his naturalistic standpoint. In fact, part of what Hume is doing is presenting a naturalistic account of how beliefs in miracles arise and, having arisen, how they affect human behavior.

30. See, for example, Ahern (1975, 20) and Levine (1988, 146).

31. See *Treatise* (*THN*, 1.3.13.4–6). Ahern (1975, 19) makes this same point.

32. Both Ahern and Levine argue for a stronger similarity between Tillotson's actual argument and Hume's actual argument, claiming that the notion of *evidential impossibility* is central to both. While it is certainly right to attribute such an argument to Tillotson, if what I have argued is correct, it is a fundamental error to attribute such an argument to Hume. See Ahern (1975, 29), Levine (1988, 154–57), and Levine (1989, 145 ff.).

References

Ahern, Dennis M. 1975. "Hume on the Evidential Impossibility of Miracles." In *Studies in Epistemology*, edited by N. Rescher. Oxford: Basil Blackwell.

Arnauld, Antoine, and Pierre Nicole. 1996. *Logic or the Art of Thinking*. Translated by Jill Vance Buroker. Edited by K. Ameriks and D. M. Clarke. *Cambridge Texts in the History of Philosophy*. Cambridge: Cambridge University Press.

Coady, C.A.J. 1992. *Testimony: A Philosophical Study*. Oxford: Oxford University Press.

Earman, John. 2000. *Hume's Abject Failure: The Argument against Miracles*. Oxford New York: Oxford University Press.

Edwards, Paul, ed. 1967. *Encyclopedia of Philosophy*. New York: Macmillan.

Fogelin, Robert J. 1985. *Hume's Skepticism in the Treatise of Human Nature*. London: Routledge and Kegan Paul.

———. 1990. "What Hume Actually Said about Miracles." *Hume Studies* 16 (1): 81–86.

———. 1992. *Philosophical Interpretations*. Oxford and New York: Oxford University Press.

———. 1994. *Pyrrhonian Reflections on Knowledge and Justification*. Oxford and New York: Oxford University Press.

Garrett, Don. 1997. *Cognition and Commitment in Hume's Philosophy*. New York and Oxford: Oxford University Press.

Hume, David. 1932. *The Letters of David Hume*. Edited by J.Y.T. Grieg. Vol. 2. Oxford: Clarendon Press.

———. 1975. *Enquiries concerning the Human Understanding and concerning the Principles of Morals*. Edited by L. A. Selby-Bigge and P. H. Nidditch. 3d ed. Oxford: Clarendon Press.

———. 1978. *A Treatise of Human Nature*. Edited by L. A. Selby-Bigge and P. H. Nidditch. 2d ed. Oxford: Oxford University Press.

Hume, David. 1999. *An Enquiry concerning Human Understanding*. Edited by Tom L. Beauchamp. Oxford: Oxford University Press.

———. 2000. *A Treatise of Human Nature*. Edited by David Fate Norton and Mary J. Norton. Oxford: Oxford University Press.

Johnson, David. 1999. *Hume, Holism, and Miracles*. Ithaca: Cornell University Press.

Levine, Michael. 1988. "Belief in Miracles: Tillotson's Argument against Transubstantiation as a Model for Hume." *International Journal for the Philosophy of Religion* 23:125–60.

———. 1989. *Hume and the Problem of Miracles: a Solution*. Dordrecht, Netherlands, and Boston: Kluwer Academic.

Lewis, C. S. 1947. *Miracles: A Preliminary Study*. New York: Macmillan.

Locke, John. 1979. *An Essay concerning Human Understanding*. Edited by P. H. Nidditch. Oxford: Clarendon Press.

Middleton, Conyers. 1749. *A Free Inquiry into Miraculous Powers, Which are supposed to have subsisted in the Christian Church, From the Earliest Ages through several successive Centuries*. London: Manby and Cox, on Ludgate Hill.

Mura, Alberto. 1996. *Dal noto all ignoto: Causalita e induzione nel pensiero di David Hume*. Filosofia, Nuova Serie. Pisa: Edizioni ETS.

———. 1998. "Hume's Inductive Logic." *Synthese* 115 (3): 303–31.

Owen, David. 1987. "Hume versus Price on Miracles and Prior Probabilities: Testimony and Baysean Calculation." *Philosophical Quarterly* 37 (147): 187–202.

Powell, William Samuel. 1776. *Discourses on Various Subjects*. London: Thomas Balguy.

Quine, W. V. 1973. *The Roots of Reference*. La Salle, Ill.: Open Court.

Sobel, J. H. 1987. "On the Evidence of Testimony for Miracles: A Bayesian Interpretation of David Hume's Analysis." *Philosophical Quarterly* 37 (147): 166–86.

Tillotson, John. 1742. *Works*. 9th ed. Dublin: George Grierson.

Tversky, Amos, and Daniel Kahneman. 1982. "Belief in the Law of Small Numbers." In *Judgments under Uncertainty: Heuristics and Biases*, edited by Daniel Kahneman, Paul Slovic, and Amos Tversky. Cambridge: Cambridge University Press.

Warburton, William. 1841. *A Selection from Unpublished Papers of the Right Reverend William Warburton*. Edited by F. Kilvert. London: John Boyer Nichols and Son.

Index